Breakfast Table Chat

BREAKFAST TABLE CHAT

BY
EDGAR A. GUEST.

DETROIT, MICH. 1914

MARSCHNER

AUTHOR'S NOTE

Acknowledgment is hereby made of the courtesy of the publishers of
Judge for permission to reprint in this book the verses "A Boy at Christmas."

A BOOK of verse is like a child—
    Its moods and fancies vary;
At times its ways are meek and mild,
    At other times contrary.

And like a child, it sometimes shows
    A charm that naught can smother;
For that, of course, the credit goes
    Entirely to its mother.

So readers, take my little lad,
    And may he be no bother;
And when you find that he is bad,
    Just blame it on his father.

356305

To

THE DETROIT FREE PRESS

As a slight expression of gratitude
this book is dedicated.

CONTENTS

BREAKFAST TABLE CHAT

BY
EDGAR A. GUEST.

DETROIT, MICH. 1914

MARSCHNER

BREAKFAST TABLE CHAT

The Green of Michigan

I'VE seen the Rockies in the west,
    I've seen the canyons wild and grim,
    I've seen the prairies golden dressed,
    And California's hedges prim.
I've seen the Kansas corn fields blow,
    I've seen them wearing summer's tan;
But there's no place on earth can show
    Such glorious green as Michigan.

I've seen the blue of foreign skies,
    I've seen old England's shady lanes,
The famous spots men advertise,
    The mountains and the rolling plains;
But wearily my eyes have turned
    From scenes that others gayly scan,
And secretly my soul has yearned
    To see the green of Michigan.

I've traveled in a Pullman car
    And watched the landscape slipping by,
But always though I've wandered far
    To fairer charms my mind would fly;
And when at last the moving scenes
    Seem painted by some Master Man
With all the cool and restful greens,
    I know I'm back in Michigan.

Here Mother Nature never tires
    And droops her head upon her breast;
Beneath the scorching summer fires
    She keeps her youth and looks her best.
When other states have lost the hue
    They had when first the spring began,
'Tis like refreshing drink to view
    The splendid green of Michigan.

Go search for charms on foreign shores,
    Enthüse of wonders, as you roam,
I choose the splendors at our doors,
    I sing the rich delights of home,
The trees in garb of glory dressed,
    The fertile fields that round us span;
I sing the charm that thrills me best,
    The glorious green of Michigan!

A Prayer

LORD, give me strength for my burdens today,
    Let me bear what is mine unafraid,
    Let me stand, head erect and face front to
        the fray
Nor call to my brothers for aid.

I ask not for easier pathways to tread
    Nor easier burdens to bear,
But I pray for the courage to journey ahead,
    And alone I would conquer my care.

Lord, make me strong for the tasks of today,
    Let me master them all if I can,
And if I must falter and fall by the way
    I pray I may fall as a man.

Friends

THE sunshine and blue skies are fine,
  I'm thankful for the flowers,
  For they are truly gifts divine
To cheer this world of ours.
But flowers droop and skies turn gray
  And oft the sunshine ends;
God's greatest blessings, so I say,
  Are friends.

The river gently flowing by,
  The rolling meadows green,
The mountains towering to the sky,
  The valleys in between
Are all a part of God's great scheme
  On which our joy depends;
But greatest of them all, I deem
  Our friends.

When sorrow comes and grief is mine,
  And hope is lost in gloom,
'Tis then that friendship comes to shine
  Within my darkened room.
'Tis then that consolation sweet
  My bitter woe attends,
For God has made this world complete
  With friends.

Good friends! God's greatest gift to man,
  That's how they seem to me,
The keystone of His wondrous plan
  To cheer humanity.
Out of His mercy infinite
  I hold the best he sends
To fill this world with love and light—
  Are friends.

The Painter

WHEN my hair is thin and silvered, an' my time
　　　of toil is through,
　　When I've many years behind me, an' ahead
　　　of me a few,
I shall want to sit, I reckon, sort of dreamin' in the sun,
An' recall the roads I've traveled an' the many things
　　　I've done,
An' I hope there'll be no picture that I'll hate to look
　　　upon
When the time to paint it better or to wipe it out is
　　　gone.

I hope there'll be no vision of a hasty word I've said,
That has left a trail of sorrow, like a whip welt, sore
　　　an' red,
An' I hope my old-age dreamin' will bring back no
　　　bitter scene
Of a time when I was selfish an' a time when I was
　　　mean;
When I'm gettin' old an' feeble, an' I'm far along
　　　life's way
I don't want to sit regrettin' any by-gone yesterday.

I'll admit the children boss me, I'll admit I often smile
When I ought to frown upon 'em, but for such a little
　　　while
They are naughty, romping youngsters, that I have
　　　no heart to scold,
An' I know if I should whip 'em I'd regret it when
　　　I'm old.
Age to me would be a torment an' a ghost-infested
　　　night,
If I'd ever hurt a baby, an' I could not make it right.

I am painting now the pictures that I'll some day
　　　want to see,
I am filling in a canvas that will come back soon to me.

18

An' though nothing great is on it, an' though nothing
    there is fine,
I shall want to look it over when I'm old an' call it
    mine.
An' I do not dare to leave it, while the paint isw arm
    an' wet,
With a single thing upon it that I'll later on regret.

The Gentle Hand of Women Folks

THE gentle hand of women folks
    Keeps this old world in line,
    It smooths away our bits of care
And makes the struggle fine.
It turns to blue our skies of gray,
    It makes our burdens lighter,
And when we feel its soft caress
    Life's gloomy spots grow brighter.

The gentle hand of women folks,
    Of sister, wife or mother,
Is what makes honest, sturdy men
    Of husband, son or brother.
It keeps man fighting to be good,
    It cheers him up in sorrow,
It gives him courage to await
    The fortunes of tomorrow.

The gentle hand of women folks,
    To kindness ever turning,
Soothing with patient tenderness
    The brow with fever burning.
Man's best reward for all the strife,
    His richest worldly blessing,
The gentle hand of women folks,
    Akin to God's caressing.

Sticky Fingers

WIFE says that I should be ashamed
    To wear such garments as I do,
    Full many a time has she exclaimed:
"A month ago that suit was new,
Now look at all the dreadful stains
    That mar the coat and spoil the vest;
It seems to me if you'd take pains
    Your clothing wouldn't get so messed."

But I am proud of all those stains,
    I do not care for garments clean,
For every shining mark explains
    Where sticky little hands have been;
Each smudge is but a symbol of
    A roguish youngster's fond caress,
A badge of trusting, constant love,
    A token of real happiness.

I may be careless in my way,
    Perhaps my clothes are a disgrace,
But when that baby comes to play
    And holds me in her fond embrace
I love her sticky fingers more
    Than any tailored suit of mine,
And she may thumb my garments o'er,
    For every spot she leaves is fine.

I wish no spotless coat and vest,
    If baby hands I have to check;
It matters not how I am dressed,
    I want her arms about my neck.
Yes, finger-marked my clothes may be,
    But they are marks I'm proudest of,
Let sticky fingers come to me
    And stamp me with their seals of love.

Cornered

I KNEW it was comin', I'd watched fer a year
　　Without sayin' a word to a soul excep' Ma
　　Of the sweet sort o' things that were happenin'
　　　　here,
　　An,' "You orter feel mighty glad of it, Pa!"
Was all that she said.　But I didn't somehow,
　　I'd a feelin' that only old men understand,
I knew it was comin'.　And it's happened now!
　　An' I answered yes, when he ast fer her hand.

I dodged him six weeks, now it's done, I confess.
　　I contrived it so's he'd never get me alone,
I knew all the time that he wanted our Bess,
　　An' that he was eager to make his wants known.
But he got me last night, passed me out a see-gar
　　An' while he was talkin' I looked at the band,
I knew in my heart that he wouldn't get far
　　Afore he'd get courage an' ask fer her hand.

An' I shook like a man with the ague, I guess,
　　Like a fellow must feel when they've doomed him
　　　　to die,
An' I didn't look up when I answered him yes,
　　I was almost ashamed of the tears in each eye.
He's honest and clean, he's a man through and through
　　An' as soon as I got my old heart in command,
I said: "Since it must be, I am glad it is you,
　　I give you my best when I give you her hand."

I knew it was comin'.　For months I could see
　　It was love that was lightin' those young people's
　　　　eyes,
And so when he finally did corner me
　　I know what he said wasn't any surprise.
Now Ma's kissin' 'em both, then she'll come out and
　　　　cry,
　　An' tomorrow she'll tell me it's perfectly grand;
Oh, happy young man, mebbe some day you'll sigh
　　When you're asked to part with your little one's
　　　　hand.

Mary

SHE was gentle, she was true,
　　And her tender eyes of blue
　　　Seemed to mock the morning sunbeams
And the starlight of the night;
And her laughter seemed to trill
Like the ripple of the rill,
And there never was a trouble
That she didn't make all right.

What though rough had been my way,
And the bitter hours of day
Had depressed my coward spirit
Till it only saw the gloom,
She could lift me from the strife
And bring back the joy of life,
For her smiling presence brightened
And made radiant the room.

Oh, so simple were her ways,
Oh, so merry were the days
That we trod life's lane together
Hand in hand, like children gay;
But my troubles seem to be
Mountain high today to me
For there are no happy evenings
When we laugh them all away.

Now the sunbeams dance and smile,
But I'm looking all the while
For the soft blue eyes of Mary
Who has passed beyond the night;
But I bravely tread my way
For I know there'll come a day
When she'll laugh away my sorrows
And make all my burdens light.

A Suggestion

IF you've grumbled through the day
  Without driving care away,
  If in spite of all your grouches
Troubles on you have kept piling;
If regardless of your kicking
And your cussing, they're still sticking,
Why not switch your tactics, mister,
And try smiling?

If your frowning will not chase 'em,
Why not grin a bit, and face 'em?
If your worries seem to like it
When your meanness they are riling;
If your gloomy disposition
Doesn't better your condition,
Why not switch your methods, mister,
And try smiling?

If your constant whining, swearing,
Do not better your wayfaring;
If you find your foes no kinder
After them you've been reviling;
If they keep right on assailing,
Quite regardless of your wailing,
Why not switch your style of warfare
And try smiling?

The Responsibility of Fatherhood

BEFORE you came, my little lad,
    I used to think that I was good,
Some vicious habits, too, I had,
But wouldn't change them if I could.
I held my head up high and said:
    "I'm all that I have need to be,
It matters not what path I tread,"
    But that was ere you came to me.

I treated lightly sacred things,
    And went my way in search of fun,
Upon myself I kept no strings,
    And gave no heed to folly done.
I gave myself up to the fight
    For worldly wealth and earthly fame,
And sought advantage, wrong or right,
    But that was long before you came.

But now you sit across from me,
    Your big brown eyes are opened wide,
And every deed I do you see,
    And, O, I dare not step aside.
I've shaken loose from habits bad,
    And what is wrong I've come to dread,
Because I know, my little lad,
    That you will follow where I tread.

I want those eyes to glow with pride,
    In me I want those eyes to see
The while we wander side by side
    The sort of man I'd have you be.
And so I'm striving to be good
    With all my might, that you may know
When this great world is understood,
    What pleasures are worth while below.

I see life in a different light
    From what I did before you came,
Then anything that pleased seemed right;
    But you are here to bear my name,
And you are looking up to me
    With those big eyes from day to day,
And I'm determined not to be
    The means of leading you astray.

Trustful Ma

MA has every confidence in Pa,
    She says she knows he always does what's
        right,
He's not at all like some folks' husbands are,
    Whose conduct very often is a fright.
She says that she can trust him anywhere
    An' know he'd never think of doing wrong,
But when he meets a widow, young an' fair,
    Ma never leaves them chatting very long.

Ma never has a single doubt of Pa,
    An' she is very thankful, too, for that;
She says she knows he'd never go too far,
    Besides, he's growing old an' bald an' fat.
But just the same when we have friends for tea,
    An' Ma has shown 'em where their places are,
Although she trusts him most implicitly
    She never puts the pretty girls by Pa.

Slumberland Time

IT is Slumberland time, and the storms have
    passed by,
       And the sea is now golden and still,
And the big yellow moon has come up in the sky,
    And the Sandman is home from the hill.
The fairy boat waits for my baby to start
    For the wonderful harbor of dreams,
Where there's never a care for the dear little heart
    And the world is as bright as it seems.

It is Slumberland time, and the sighing is done,
    The hurts of the day are all well,
The wee childish troubles all passed with the sun,
    Now the Sandman is ringing his bell.
The big yellow moon lights the way with his beams
    To the land where my baby shall go,
Where the night time's a round of most wonderful
       dreams
    And there's never a sorrow to know.

It is Slumberland time, and the tears are all dried,
    And the dream ship is putting to sea,
My baby must sail o'er the rest-ocean wide
    Till the morn brings her safely to me.
Toss gently, O Slumberland breezes, her curls,
    Be kind to her, fairies, I pray,
Let never a sad dream be my little girl's
    Till the sunbeams shall call her to play.

Grandma

THERE'S a twinkle in her eye,
  O, so merry! O, so sly!
    That you never see the wrinkles in her face;
She's so full of fun and play
That you never see the gray
In her tresses, and you never see a trace
Of the feebleness of years,
Born of heartaches and of tears;
She's the youngest of the children still today.
All the charm of youth remains,
All her beauty she retains.
O, she's right up to the minute in her way.

Just because she's seventy-two
Any old thing will not do,
She believes that she must always look her best;
Though her gowns are mostly black,
She was never known to lack
A little dash of color at her breast.
"Just because I'm old," says she,
"Do not think I'm going to be
 Out of style and frumpy looking, for I'm not!
And when folks come in to call,
I'm not going to wear a shawl
And cover up the splendid things I've got."

O, dear grandma, let me say,
As I look at you today,
In your stylish gown of satin with its little touch of
      blue;
As I see your merry eye,
When the years have wandered by
May I only be as happy and as lovable as you.
May I come from out the gloom
Of my troubles with the bloom
Of a heart that's ever youthful still in view,
With a dash of color gay
To relieve the somber gray,
May I be as young as you at seventy-two.

The Little Country Bus

THERE'S no lock upon your door,
        And the polish that you wore
        In the years ago when you were bright
                and new
Now has lost its splendid shine,
And your driver's bending spine
Shows that he's been getting old along with you.
You are slipping fast, I see;
So indeed, old bus, is he;
But you rattle and you bang along the street,
And I wonder as you go
What of joy or what of woe
You'll discover when the limited you meet.

Who is coming home once more
To his father's welcome door?
Is it failure or success that he will bring?
Is a daughter slipping back
From the city's cruel track
For the lullaby that mother used to sing?
Is she happy?   Is she sad?
For I know, old bus, you've had
Both your passengers a thousand times or more;
And old driver, you can't hide
Just how many times you've sighed
As you've opened or have shut that shaky door.

You have seen them go away,
Full of strength and hope and gay,
You have seen them start as children fine—and
                then—
When the limited you've met,
Both your kindly eyes were wet
As you saw them back as women and as men.
You have read the tale of life,
Read the heartache and the strife,
Read the sorrows that we'd better not discuss,
Read the joy of splendid things
And the pain that failure brings,
As you've carried all that's human in your bus.

28

So I wonder as you go
What you'll find of joy or woe
When the limited pulls in on time today;
What of conquest or defeat
Will it be your lot to meet
And to welcome in your gentle, kindly way.
Both your shaky bus and you
With life's toil are nearly through,
Soon your soul upon a journey far will roam;
And I like to think you'll ask
God to let it be your task
To welcome all the children coming home.

The Man Who's Down

IT is well enough to cheer for the brother who
is up,
It is fine to praise the brother who has cap-
tured victory's cup;
But don't keep your kind words always for the man
who's won renown,
For the boy who really needs them is the fellow who is
down.

Give a cheer when men deserve it, shout your praise
for them to hear,
Don't reserve your admiration till a man is on his bier,
But remember as you wander every day about the
town
That a kind word will work wonders for the brother
who is down.

For the man on top is happy, and he has a thousand
friends,
He can always get a kind word, no matter where he
wends,
But the brother who is striving to attain a laurel crown
Often needs a friend to help him. Don't neglect the
brother down.

A Breach of Friendship

'TIS friendship's test to guard the name
    Of him you love from all attack,
    As you are to his face, the same
To be when you're behind his back.

Now good old loyal Jimmy Green,
A traitor to you have I been;
As false as Arnold to my trust,
Your name I've trampled in the dust.
Last night I lingered out till two,
And said that I had been with you,
And then straightway my wife began
To prove to me that you're no man.
"What, out again," said she, "with Green!
No decent man with him is seen!
No man who valued much his home
With him would ever care to roam,
But for the children, long ago
His own wife would have quit, I know;
His only friends are loafers, who
Don't care what vicious things they do;
He'd steal, he'd lie, he's insincere."
And all I said was: "Yes, my dear."

"Who else was with you, tell me pray?
Come, answer me, and right away!"
And then I muttered, "Freddie Brown,"
And promptly turned poor Freddie down.
"What, Brown," she screamed, "that low-down thing
Who all his life has had his fling!
That selfish brute who doesn't care
What shabby clothes his wife must wear
So long as he can spend his pay
And turn the night hours into day!
I'd never go about the town
And tell that I had been with Brown;
I've always said his hang-dog look
Betrayed the fact that he's a crook.
And you with him! Of all men, you!
I wonder now what next you'll do?

30

You know Fred Brown's a man to fear."
And all I said was: "Yes, my dear."

"Who else was with you all this night?"
She asked, and I said, "Billy White."
And Billy White was next to fall
Before her rhetoric in the hall.
I don't remember now just what
She said of Bill, but 'twas a lot.
Perhaps I should have argued back,
And spared my friends from her attack.
Perhaps I should have pointed out
That they are men beyond all doubt,
Men who have won their share of fame,
That each one bears an honored name.
Perhaps I should have argued there
And proved her charges most unfair;
But it was two, as I have said,
And I was tired and wished for bed;
So by the short route chose to steer,
And all I said was: "Yes, my dear."

Riches

IF I can leave behind me here and there
    A friend or two to say when I am gone
    That I had helped to make their pathways fair,
Had brought them smiles when they were bowed with
        care,
    The riches of this world I'll carry on.

If only three or four shall pause to say,
    When I have passed beyond this earthly sphere,
That I brought gladness to them on a day
When bitterness was their's, I'll take away
    More riches than a billionaire leaves here.

Down the Lanes of August

DOWN the lanes of August—and the bees upon
  the wing,
    All the world's in color now, and all the
      song birds sing;
Never reds will redder be, more golden be the gold,
Down the lanes of August, and the summer getting
  old.

Mother Nature's brushes now with paints are dripping
  wet,
Gorgeous is her canvas with the tints we can't forget;
Here's a yellow wheat field—purple asters there,
Riotous the colors that she's splashing everywhere.

Red the cheeks of apples and pink the peaches' bloom,
Redolent the breezes with the sweetness of perfume;
Everything is beauty crowned by skies of clearest
  blue,
Mother Earth is at her best once more for me and
  you.

Down the lanes of August with her blossoms at our
  feet,
Rich with gold and scarlet, dripping wet with honey
  sweet.
Rich or poor, no matter, here are splendors spread
Down the lanes of August, for all who wish to tread.

Little Miss Laugh-a-Lot

LITTLE Miss Laugh-a-Lot,
  Saucy the way you've got,
    Dancing with glee are the bright eyes of
  you;
Lips like the red, red rose,
Cunning, your little nose,
Cheeks like the summer peach sparkling with dew;
Mischievous romping tot,
Little Miss Laugh-a-Lot,
Over this heart of mine you've worked a spell,
You've got me, heart and soul,
Under your sly control,
In that glad smile of yours all my joys dwell.

Little Miss Laugh-a-Lot,
Merry the way you've got,
What you say goes with your battered old dad.
Kings, in their pompous way,
Hold no such magic sway
Over their subjects, as you've always had;
Your word is law with me,
Your throne, you've made my knee,
Empress, you rule me by night and by day.
By you I'm always swayed,
Your commands I've obeyed,
Always I'm ready when you bid me play.

Little Miss Laugh-a-Lot,
Roguish the ways you've got,
Sly are the tricks that you play on your dad,
Wheedling and coaxing him,
Fooling and hoaxing him,
Forcing this grizzly old bear to be glad.
Life holds no sweeter bliss
Than your caress and kiss,
Earth has no beauty so rare as your smile,
While I have you to love,
You to be servant of,
Nothing else matters, this world is worth while.

Song of the Many

THIS is the song of the many
    Who seldom are mentioned in praise,
    The glorious millions of toilers
    Who splendidly live out their days.
The millions unlured by great riches,
    Uneager for fame or applause,
Not seeking for history's niches,
    Forever upholding a cause;
The many who bravely are bearing
    The duties of life, as they plod,
Contentedly, gayly wayfaring
    With faith in their country and God.

The millions, unnoticed, unheeded,
    Who cheerfully tramp to and fro;
Always found at their posts when they're needed,
    Not seeking for glamour or show.
Good fathers, devoted and tender,
    And rightfully proud of their young,
Yes, these are the men that engender
    The spirit that ought to be sung.
Men who live for the dear ones who love them,
    Their happiness being their goal,
Yes, these, though we hear little of them,
    Are the men that we ought to extol.

But few in the world attain glory,
    But few ever sink in disgrace,
Compared to the ones who grow hoary
    In quietly filling a place.
In unselfishly, splendidly living,
    And honestly facing life's test;
The many who daily are giving
    The world every bit of their best.
Yes, these are the men I would sing to,
    The many who cheerfully plod
O'er life's highway, contented to cling to
    Their faith in their country and God.

The Ballad of the New Arrival

IT isn't the blue in the skies,
    Nor the song of the whispering trees,
    The light in a fair maiden's eyes,
My joy is far greater than these;
You will pardon my arrogance please,
    And forgive the wide bulge in my brow,
My hand I'll permit you to seize,
    There's another to welcome me now.

Naught to me are political cries,
    Or Teddy's or Taft's policies;
The charges of fraud or of lies,
    Or Wilson's big stock of degrees.
Pinning blankets, long dresses, boot-ees
    This morning are all I allow
In my thoughts, both at work and at ease,
    There's another to welcome me now.

With a smile on my face I arise,
    And beg for permission to squeeze
The wee little hand that I prize,
    And I wonder if daddy he sees.
The world with its mountains and seas
    Is a mighty big place, but I vow,
The whole world is here at my knees,
    There's another to welcome me now.

Prince, at your pleasures I sneeze,
    You to riches and glory may bow,
But my joy is greater than these,
    There's another to welcome me now.

A Coming Reunion

JIM'S made good in the world out there, an' Kate
    has a man that's true,
      No better, of course, than she deserves; she's
      rich, but she's happy, too;
Fred is manager, full-fledged now—he's boss of a big
    concern
An' I lose my breath when I think sometimes of the
    money that he can earn;
Clever—the word don't mean enough to tell what they
    really are,
Clever, an' honest an' good an' kind—if you doubt me,
    ask their Ma.

Proud of 'em! Well, I should say we are, an' we have
    a right to be,
Some are proud to have one child, an' I am proud of
    three!
That's all the honor a fellow needs, why Ma an' I often
    say
There isn't a king or a queen on earth as proud as we
    are today;
Three babies off in the world out there, all honest an'
    kind an' true,
That's something to brag of when you are old an' your
    journey is almost through.

We've stretched the table out a bit, the way that it
    used to be,
When we were younger—an' here's Ma's chair, an'
    there is a place for me;
An' there's a chair for our little Kate an' one for the
    man she wed,
An' yonder, just to the left of Ma, is a place for our
    baby Fred,
An' Jim, the eldest, will sit by me—they're comin'
    Thanksgiving day
To sit once more where they used to sit before they
    went away.

They ain't ashamed of the old, old place, an' they
    ain't ashamed of me,
An' they're just as proud of their dear old Ma as ever
    they used to be;
They've got rich friends in the city now, an' there's
    nothing that's fine they lack,
But their hearts still stay with us here at home, and
    they joy in the comin' back.
So we've stretched the table out a bit to the length
    that it was when they
Were youngsters here in the home with us. They're
    comin' Thanksgiving day.

The Right to Joy

I DO not ask for roses all the time,
    For blue skies bending o'er me every day,
    I do not ask for easy hills to climb,
And always for my feet a pleasant way.
In laughter I would not spend all my life,
    And miss the joy of sweet and sacred pain;
I want to know life's burden and its strife,
    And feel upon my cheek the splash of rain.

I merely pray for strength enough to bear
    My burdens, and to tread the rugged way;
To keep the right, howe'er beset with care,
    To stand, unflinching, face front, to the fray.
And I would claim life's roses for my own,
    But I would win my right to know their sweet;
To level paths I'd march my way alone,
    For victory I'd venture with defeat.

Temptation

"I WOULD like to wed your daughter," said the
multi-millionaire,
"I will try to make her happy; if I don't you
needn't care;
She shall have five million dollars just the minute
we are married;
Say the word and I will take her"—but the maiden's
father tarried.

"Every luxury I'll give her, she shall dress in finest
raiment
And the moment we are married I shall make the
wedding payment;
She'll be worth five million dollars when the wedding
vows are said,
Will you say that it's a bargain?"—but the father
hung his head.

"It is true I'm almost fifty and your daughter's scarce
eighteen.
But she'll live a life of splendor, she shall be a social
queen;
She shall dine with kings and princes and by royalty
be favored,
And she'll have five million dollars"—here the
tempted father wavered.

Oh! I would that I could write it, that before the
father's eyes
Came the picture of the baby that he'd learned to
idolize;
Came his little girl at evening for a romp upon his
knee,
Came the little roguish lassie of the days that used
to be.

Had there come that very moment when he saw the
rich man's check
Just a vision of his baby with her arms about his
neck;

Had his eyes turned back one minute to the days of
    long ago,
Then he never would have wavered—he'd have fairly
    shouted: "No."

A Preference

I'D rather be considered dull
    Than use my brain denouncing things;
    I'd rather not be critical
      And utter words that carry stings.
I'd rather never speak at all
    Than speak as one who seems to feel
That other's faults, howe'er so small,
    It proves him clever to reveal.

I have no wish to pose on earth
    As born to judge my fellow men;
I'd rather praise them for their worth;
    If failures, bid them try again.
If faulty effort I behold,
    In silence, let me pass it by,
If I must leave it unextolled,
    At least the toiler shall not sigh.

No reputation would I gain
    For wisdom, if in gaining it
I cause some humble worker pain
    And wound him by my flash of wit.
There is no cleverness in sneers,
    A fool can scoff in manner pert;
Great wisdom by this test appears
    In never saying things that hurt.

The Evening Prayer

LITTLE girlie, kneeling there,
    Speaking low your evening prayer,
    In your cunning little nightie
With your pink toes peeping through;
With your eyes closed and your hands
Tightly clasped, while daddy stands
In the doorway, just to hear the
"God bless papa," lisped by you.
You don't know just what I feel,
As I watch you nightly kneel
By your trundle bed and whisper
Soft and low your little prayer!
But in all I do or plan,
I'm a bigger, better man
Every time I hear you asking
God to make my journey fair.

Little girlie, kneeling there,
Lisping low your evening prayer,
Asking God above to bless me,
At the closing of each day;
Oft the tears come to my eyes,
And I feel a big lump rise
In my throat, that I can't swallow,
And I sometimes turn away.
In the morning, when I wake,
And my post of duty take,
I go forth with new-born courage
To accomplish what is fair;
And throughout the live-long day,
I am striving every way
To come back to you each evening
And be worthy of your prayer.

When It's Bad to Forget

DID you ever meet a brother as you hurried on
your way
And invite him up to dinner, and his wife;
Did you ever keep him standing until he had named
the day
When you'd meet to talk about your early life?
Did you ever say: "Next Tuesday we'll expect you
up to dine,"
And repeat it so he'd have no cause to doubt it?
Did you ever make him promise to come up and taste
your wine,
And then forget to tell your wife about it?

Did you ever get home feeling just as happy as a bird,
Kiss your smiling wife and settle down to tea,
And then get a sinking feeling in your insides as you
heard
The door bell ring? This has occurred to me.
Has a single pork chop lying on a cold and greasy dish
Ever furiously set your heart to drumming,
As your guests arrived that evening in obedience to
your wish,
And you hadn't told your wife that they were
coming?

Oh, I do not care for riches, and I do not sigh for fame,
And I do not yearn for glory or for power,
And I don't care if I never learn to win a billiard game
At the present rate of 40 cents an hour.
With my lot I'd be contented, and I know I'd happy
be
And I'd go my way a bit of music humming,
If I only could remember when I ask folks up for tea
To inform my darling wife that they are coming.

Mothers' Splendid Dreams

MOTHERS dream such splendid dreams when
their little babies smile,
Dreams of wondrous deeds they'll do in
the happy after-while;
Every mother of a boy knows that in her arms is curled
One who some day will arise splendidly to serve the
world.

Mothers sing their babes to sleep, weaving through
their lullabies
Visions of true-hearted men when their sons to man-
hood rise;
Greatness slumbers in the cot that each mother guards
with care,
And the world she knows will be better for her baby
fair.

Mothers dream such splendid dreams of the men that
are to be
In the years that are to come glorious are the things
they see;
None so poor and none so frail but looks yonder down
life's lane
And sees there the splendid hights that her baby
will attain.

Mothers dream such splendid dreams, that no matter
what we do
We can never hope to make half their visionings come
true;
Always, as they look ahead, down the lane of life
they see
Greater men than yet have been in the men that are
to be.

Patriotism

I THINK my country needs my vote,
    I know it doesn't need my throat,
        My lungs and larynx, too;
And so I sit at home at night
And teach my children what is right
        And wise for them to do;
And when I'm on the job by day
I do my best to earn my pay.

The arguments may rage and roar,
I grease the hinges on my door
        And paint the porches blue; ·
I love this splendid land of ours,
And so I plant the seeds and flowers
        And watch them bursting through.
I never stand upon a box
To say we're headed for the rocks.

My notion of a patriot
Is one who guards his little cot,
        And keeps it up to date;
Who pays his taxes when they're due,
And pays his bills for groc'ries, too,
        And dresses well his mate;
He keeps his children warmly clad
And lets them know they have a dad.

The nation's safe as long as men
Get to their work and back again
        Each day with cheerful smile;
So long as there are fathers who
Rejoice in what they have to do
        And find their homes worth while,
The Stars and Stripes will wave on high
And liberty will never die.

The Change-Worker

A FELLER don't start in t' think of himself an'
  the part that he's playin' down here
  When there's nobody lookin' t' him fer sup-
port, an' he don't give a thought t' next year.
His faults don't seem big an' his habits not worse than
  a whole lot of others he knows,
An' he don't seem t' care what his neighbors may
  think as heedlessly forward he goes.
He don't start t' think if it's wrong or it's right, with
  his speech he is careless or glib
Till the minute the nurse lets him into the room t' see
  what's asleep in the crib.

An' then as he looks at that bundle o' red, at the wee
  little fingers an' toes
An' he knows it's his flesh an' his bone that is there, an'
  will be just like him when it grows,
It comes in a flash t' a feller right then, there is more
  here than pleasure or pelf,
An' the sort of a man his baby will be is the sort of a
  man he's himself.
Then he kisses the mother an' kisses the child, an' goes
  out determined that he
Will endeavor t' be just the sort of a man that he
  wants his baby t' be.

A feller don't think that it matters so much what he
  does till a baby arrives,
He sows his wild oats an' he has his gay fling an' head-
  long in pleasure he dives;
An' a drink more or less doesn't matter much then, for
  life is a comedy gay,
But the moment a crib is put up in the home an' a
  baby has come there t' stay
He thinks of the things he has done in the past, an' it
  strikes him as hard as a blow,
That the path he has trod in the past is a path that he
  don't want his baby t' go.

I ain't much t' preach, an' I can't just express in the
    way that your clever men can
The thoughts that I think, but it seems t' me now that
    when God wants t' rescue a man
From himself an' the follies that harmless appear, but
    which, under the surface, are grim,
He summons the angel of infancy sweet, an' sends
    down a baby t' him.
For in that way He opens his eyes t' himself, and He
    gives him the vision t' see
That his duty's t' be just the sort of a man that he's
    wantin' his baby t' be.

Faith

GOD never yet has sent a care
    Too great for mortal man to bear,
    Nor from the cradle to the tomb
Kept wanderers in perpetual gloom;
But He has strewn our time of years
With laughter and with scalding tears,
And if it's ours to mourn today
Should we not bravely keep the way?

God would not always have us play,
Nor ever dance along life's way;
Our faith is not by sunshine tried,
But by the clouds that come to hide
The morning sun, and by our cares;
And noblest he who noblest bears,
Who sheds the tears that grief compels,
Yet ne'er against his God rebels.

The Boy and the Flag

I WANT my boy to love his home,
 His mother, yes, and me;
  I want him, whereso'er he'll roam,
With us in thought to be.
I want him to love what is fine,
 Nor let his standards drag,
But, oh, I want that boy of mine
 To love his country's flag.

I want him when he older grows
 To love all things of earth;
And oh! I want him, when he knows,
 To choose the things of worth.
I want him to the hights to climb
 Nor let ambition lag;
But, oh! I want him all the time
 To love his country's flag.

I want my boy to know the best,
 I want him to be great;
I want him in life's distant west,
 Prepared for any fate.
I want him to be simple, too,
 Though clever, ne'er to brag,
But, oh! I want him, through and through
 To love his country's flag.

I want my boy to be a man,
 And yet in distant years
I pray that he'll have eyes that can
 . Not quite keep back the tears
When, coming from some foreign shore
 And alien scenes that fag,
Borne on its native breeze, once more
 He sees his country's flag.

The Disgrace of Poverty

THE lady what comes up to our house t' wash
    Is awfully poor, an' she's got
    Three babies t' care for, an' that's why she
  works,
    An' that's why she worries a lot.
An' Ma says her husband don't help her at all,
    An' Pa says it's plainly a case
Where we should be kind t' the woman, becoz
    Real poverty ain't no disgrace.

An' yesterday mornin' I went down t' her
    An' told her what my Pa had said,
An' she started t' cry, an' she dried off her hands
    An' stooped down an' patted my head.
Then I ast if her husband worked hard like my Pa,
    Or couldn't he get work t' do,
Then she wiped off her tears an' smiled as she said:
    "What a queer little fellow are you!"

Then she told me her husband was no good at all,
    But jes' loafs around all the day,
An' that's why she comes up t' our house t' wash,
    So's she can get money t' pay
For stockin's an' things for her children t' wear,
    An' buy 'em the food that they eat;
Coz if she didn't do it the landlord would come
    An' turn 'em all into the street.

An' her husband ain't sick.   He's as strong as my Pa,
    An' I told her that I'd be ashamed
If I was so poor, not t' get out an' work,
    Unless I was crippled an' lamed.
Then she kissed me an' told me t' run out an' play,
    But I'm thinkin' as hard as I can
That sometimes it happens that poverty is
    An awful disgrace to a man.

The Graduation Dress

I'M not kicking on expenses, now the sewing time
    commences,
    I will buy chiffon and laces till they say they've
      got enough;
Sure her dress for graduation shall excite the
    admiration
    Of the masses who behold her; it shall be the
      finest stuff.
She shall even carry roses, when her high school
    training closes,
    For she's worthy of the finest that there is in all
      the town;
But I sometimes sit and ponder of the days away
    off yonder
    When her mother graduated in a simple gingham
      gown.

I have watched the fuss and bustle, and this ceaseless
    rush and hustle,
    And I've listened to the planning of this
      graduation dress,
And I know when all is ended, she will make a picture
    splendid,
    And I wouldn't be contented if she didn't, I
      confess.
But I still recall the other glorious picture of her
    mother,
    With her cheeks as pink as peaches and her hair
      a golden brown,
As I gazed at her enraptured, and my heart, I know,
    she captured
    On the day she graduated in her simple gingham
      gown.

I'd be laughed down if I said it, in such matters they
    don't credit
    Me with knowing what is really very swell;
I can picture now their faces, if instead of silk and
    laces,
    My preference for gingham, I should tell.

But with me it's grown a passion, and in spite of style
    and fashion,
    And what women folks think needful, I insist and
        write it down,
I shall never see another quite so charming as her
    mother
    On the day she graduated in her simple gingham
        gown.

Neil Snow

THE whistle sounds! The game is o'er!
    We pay our tribute now with tears
    Instead of smiling eyes and cheers.
Neil Snow has crossed the line once more.

Life's scrimmage ends! A manly soul
    Now passes bravely through the night,
    Undaunted still and Spotless White.
Neil Snow has made another goal.

The crowds depart. The setting sun
    Blazes his pathway to the west.
    The stamp of valor's on his breast.
Neil Snow the Master's M has won.

Mother of Five

SHE mothered five!
    Night after night she watched a little
        bed,
        Night after night she cooled a fevered head,
Day after day she guarded little feet,
Taught little minds the dangers of the street;
Taught little lips to utter simple prayers,
Whispered of strength that some day would be theirs
And trained them all to use it as they should.
She gave her babies to the nation's good.

She mothered five!
She gave her beauty—from her cheeks let fade
The roses' blushes—to her mother trade.
She saw the wrinkles furrowing her brow,
Yet smiling said, "My boy grows stronger now."
When pleasures called she turned away and said:
"I dare not leave my babies to be fed
By strangers' hands; besides they are so small,
I must be near to hear them when they call."

She mothered five!
Night after night they sat about her knee
And heard her tell of what some day would be.
From her they learned that in the world outside
Are cruelty and vice and selfishness and pride;
From her they learned the wrongs they ought to shun,
What things to love, what work must still be done.
She led them through the labyrinth of youth
And brought five men and women up to Truth.

She mothered five!
Her name may be unknown save to the few,
Of her the outside world but little knew;
But somewhere five are treading Virtue's ways,
Serving the world and brightening its days;
Somewhere are five, who, tempted, stand upright,
Clinging to honor, keeping her memory bright;
Somewhere this mother toils and is alive
No more as one, but in the breasts of five.

A Scare

THERE are noises that freeze up the blood,
    There's the sound of the burglar at night
    As he's picking the lock, and the thud
Of a wind-worried door I thought tight;
But there's nothing that frightens me more
    Nor causes such horrible dread
As the bumpety-bump on the floor
    When the baby falls out of his bed.

The coal pile may rattle and roll
    As it will in its uncanny way,
But I keep my nerves under control.
    The neighbor's pet canine may bay
At the moon, and I merely turn o'er,
    But I lose absolutely my head
At that bumpety-bump on the floor
    When the baby falls out of his bed.

A shot may ring out in the street,
    And "murder" a woman may yell;
I may listen to scurrying feet
    But I handle myself rather well.
A dark house I'll even explore,
    But my heart stops as though I were dead
At that bumpety-bump on the floor
    When the baby falls out of his bed.

I know that the old mothers say
    That once every baby must fall,
That they seldom are hurt in that way
    And really don't mind it at all;
But still terror closes each pore
    And my hair stands up straight on my head
At that bumpety-bump on the floor
    When the baby falls out of his bed.

The Shattered Dream

I WAS somewhere off in Europe spending money
    like a king,
Owned a yacht like J. P. Morgan's, when the
    'phone began to ring;
I was entertaining princes, dukes and earls, when wifie
    said:
"It's the telephone that's ringing, you must hustle
    out of bed."
And I wandered down the stairway, grumbling o'er
    my vanished joy,
Growled: "Hello;" and then he shouted: "You're an
    uncle! It's a boy!"

I was dazed for half a minute—when you're cruising
    foreign seas
With a lot of royal people, and your sails are full of
    breeze,
And your guests are gaily laughing, and your skies
    are blue above,
The arrival of a baby isn't what you're thinking of;
And I hardly knew I'd taken that old 'phone receiver
    down
When excitedly he shouted: "There's a junior come
    to town!"

But I traveled back from Europe just as quickly as I
    could,
And left those dukes and princes and I shouted to
    him: "Good!"
I fired my stylish butlers and I threw my yacht away,
In my dollar-blue-pajamas I stood there and cried:
    "Hooray!"
I quit the king, not caring that my conduct might
    annoy,
And I shouted up to mother: "Did you hear me?
    It's a boy!"

When I'm dreaming I am wealthy and with money
    I am free,
There are times I do not welcome folks who telephone
    to me;

But I don't begrudge the finest dream that ever
    sweetened sleep
To one who has such news as that, great news that
    cannot keep.
He may wake me any moment, and my peace it
    won't destroy,
For I'll share his gladness with him, when he tells me:
    "It's a boy!"

A Creed

I MAY suffer,
    But I will not whine.
    This would I make
A creed of mine;
I may not win,
    The goal I crave,
But failing, I
    Will still be brave.

I'll do my best,
    And give my all
Unto each task,
    Then if I fall,
Battered and bruised,
    My way I'll take;
Excuses though
    I will not make.

And whether up
    Or down I go,
I wish to feel
    'Twas ordered so,
That what I am
    Is God's great plan;
But I won't fail
    To be a man.

Christmas Greeting

I DO not care to wait until the hand of death
    has smoothed your brow
    Before I say what's in my heart, I'd rather
    tell it to you now.
I'd rather say: "How glad I am to know your cheery
    voice and smile,"
Than stand and say "how glad I was" in some gri
    stricken after-while.
I'd rather shout: "how good you are!" than sniffle c
    "how good was he!"
And so I take this Christmas Day to say you have
    friend in me.

And so I take this Christmas Day to wish you every-
    thing that's fine,
A cloudless sky for every day, a path where roses
    bloom and twine;
May sorrow never find your door, but if it shall and
    leave you dumb,
May to your wounds of grief the balm of consolation
    quickly come.
May all the best of life be yours, and may, no matter
    where you roam,
Good luck and gladness go with you, and smiling,
    bring you safely home.

If wishing only banished care you'd never more have
    cause to sigh,
If wishing drove the clouds away henceforth the blue
    would fill your sky.
The pink of health would bloom upon the cheeks of
    those you love for aye,
And every day God gives to you would be a merry
    Christmas Day.
I'd wish you everything that's good, I'd wish you
    everything that's fine,
And then I'd still be in your debt, oh good and faith-
    ful friend of mine.

54

A New Year's Song

LOVE and laughter lead you
    Down the pathways of the year,
And may each morning feed you
    From the golden spoon of cheer;
May every eye be shining,
    And every cheek aglow,
And may the silver lining
    Of the clouds forever show.

May peace and plenty find you,
    May pain and grief depart;
And may you leave behind you
    The little cares that smart;
May no day be distressful,
    No night be filled with woe,
And may you be successful
    Wherever you may go.

May June bring you her roses,
    May summer poppies bloom,
And may each day that closes
    Be fragrant with perfume.
May you have no regretting
    When evening is begun,
No vain and idle fretting
    O'er what you might have done.

May envy quit your dwelling
    And hatred leave your heart;
May you rejoice in telling
    Your brother's better part.
May you be glad you're living
    However dark your way,
And find your joy in giving
    Your service to the day.

What Ma Said

WHEN Pa came home last night he had a
  package in his hand,
 "Now Ma," said he, "I've something here
 which you will say is grand.
A friend of mine got home today from hunting in the
  woods,
He's been away a week or two, and got back with the
  goods.
He had a corking string of birds, I wish you could
  have seen 'em!"
"If you've brought any partridge home," said Ma,
  "you'll have to clean 'em."

"Now listen, Ma," said Pa to her, "these birds are
  mighty rare.
I know a lot of men who'd pay a heap to get a pair.
But it's against the law to sell this splendid sort of
  game,
And if you bought 'em you would have to use a dif-
  ferent name.
It isn't every couple has a pair to eat between 'em."
"If you got any partridge there," says Ma, "you'll
  have to clean 'em."

"Whenever kings want something fine, it's partridge
  that they eat,
And millionaires prefer 'em, too, to every sort of meat.
About us everywhere tonight are folks who'd think
  it fine
If on a brace of partridge they could just sit down to
  dine.
They've got a turkey skinned to death, they're
  sweeter than a chicken."
"If that's what you've brought home," says Ma,
  "you'll have to do the pickin'."

And then Pa took the paper off and showed Ma what
    he had,
"There, look at those two beauties, don't they start
    you feelin' glad?
An' ain't your mouth a-waterin' to think how fine
    they'll be
When you've cooked 'em up for dinner, one for you
    an' one for me?"
But Ma just turned her nose up high, an' said when
    she had seen 'em,
"You'll never live to eat 'em if you wait for me to
    clean 'em."

Life

THE dog has life, the breathing ant
    Is living here, as you and I,
    And in the yard the humblest plant
Lives out its life beneath the sky.

Life, in itself, is all about,
    'Tis given not alone to man,
For life we are not singled out
    And favored by some special plan.

Life's but the opportunity
    To work and be of service here,
A thousand creatures we may see
    Who merely live from year to year.

And to the creatures we descend
    If this is all that we bequeath
Those who surround us at the end,
    That life is just the power to breathe.

Worth While

HE doesn't care that I'm not rich,
　Or that I'm poorly dressed,
　That I'm a toiler in the ditch
He hasn't even guessed.
My faults that other people know
　He doesn't even see,
For every night with eyes aglow
　He toddles up to me.

Although I'm just a common dub,
　And ordinary clay,
His cheek to mine he's glad to rub
　Before I go away;
And every night when I return,
　He's glad as he can be,
And though but little I may earn
　He toddles up to me.

To come to me he'd leave a king,
　If one were sitting near,
Unto no millionaire he'd cling
　If only I'd appear.
And though but tattered rags are mine
　When I go home to tea
With eyes that fairly beam and shine
　He'd toddle up to me.

And so I've reason to be glad,
　And reason to rejoice,
It's worth the world to be a dad,
　To be a baby's choice.
There is no prize fame can bestow,
　No joy can ever be
So real, as when, with eyes aglow,
　He toddles up to me.

The Path o' Little Children

THE path o' little children is the path I want to
    tread,
    Where green is every valley and every rose
is red,
Where laughter's always ringing and every smile is
    real,
And where the hurts are little hurts that just a kiss will
    heal.

The path o' little children, on the primrose edge o'
    life,
That leads away from jealousy and bitterness and
    strife;
The path that leads to gladness—that's the way I
    want to go,
Where no one speaks unkindly an' where no one keeps
    a foe.

The path o' little children that winds o'er hill and dale
An' leads us down to gentle seas where tiny vessels
    sail;
An' leads us through the barnyard an' through the
    pasture bars
An' brings us home at evening with hearts that know
    no scars.

The path o' little children, where peaceful dreams
    come true,
Where sunshine's always streaming, an' every sky is
    blue;
Where each one loves the other, an' every one is fair,
An' cheeks are pink with beauty, an' singing fills the
    air.

The path o' little children, it's there I want to tread,
Where innocence is dwelling with not a thing to dread;
Where care is not an ogre and sin is but a name,
An' no one thinks of money an' no one sighs for fame.

Only a Building

(Celebrating the formal dedication of the new home of the Detroit Board of Commerce.)

YOU may delve down to rock for your founda-
  tion piers,
  You may go with your steel to the sky;
You may purchase the best of the thought of the years
  And the finest of workmanship buy;
You may line with the rarest of marble each wall,
  And with gold you can tint it, but then
It is only a building if it after all
  Isn't filled with the spirit of men.

You may put up a structure of brick and of stone
  Such as never was put up before;
Place within it the costliest woods that are grown
  And carve every pillar and door;
You may fill it with splendors of quarry and mine,
  With the glories of brush and of pen;
But it's only a building, though ever so fine,
  If it hasn't the spirit of men.

You may build such a structure that lightning can't
   harm,
  Or one that an earthquake can't raze;
You may build it of granite and boast that its charm
  Shall last to the end of all days.
But you might as well never have builded at all,
  Never cleared off the bog and the fen
If after it's finished, it's sheltering wall
  Doesn't stand for the spirit of men.

For it isn't the marble, nor is it the stone,
  Nor is it the columns of steel
By which is the worth of an edifice known,
  But something that's living and real.

It isn't its grandeur that makes a place great,
    For a shack becomes glorious when
(And thousands will gladly walk up to its gate)
    It is doing a service for men.

Is it only a building you dedicate here
    With its splendors of marble and stone?
Is it only with brick and with plaster you rear,
    Or something of flesh and of bone?
Oh, vain were this building, though splendid its dress,
    And vain were its desks and its shelves
That you dedicate now to man's service, unless
    You dedicate also yourselves.

The Limit

I CAN stand for the man with the cute little bow
    On the back of his green colored hat,
    For there are a lot of good fellows I know
Who somehow have fallen for that.
The fedora of plush is a lid I don't like,
    It's a fad that will never be missed,
But somehow I've always an itching to strike
    The man with the watch on his wrist.

I've grown peevish at times at the ladylike man
    Who says "Mercy me!" and "O, dear!"
And the chap in the ball room who uses a fan
    Is the chap I could swat on the ear.
The swell with a cane in the crotch of his arm
    Isn't human, I often insist,
But some day somebody is going to harm
    The man with the watch on his wrist.

61

The Child World

THE child world is a wondrous world,
For there the flags of hate are furled,
And there the imps of wickedness
Cause neither sorrow nor distress.
And there is never strife for gold,
There petty gossip's never told,
There all is joy and wondrous mirth,
The child earth is a glorious earth.

The land of childhood is aglow
With smiles, and there pink roses grow
Upon the cheeks of boys and girls;
The golden rod is yellow curls,
And eyes of brown and eyes of blue
Are daisies and the violets, too;
And warm and true is every hand
That clings to yours in Childhood Land.

Who owns a spot on childhood's globe
Envies no king his ermine robe;
Envies no sage his manners wise,—
His world is rich with glad surprise,
The quaintest of all speech he hears,
The truest smiles, the sweetest tears
Are his possessions every day
However troubled be his way.

Who knows the joys of Childhood Land,
The pressure of a tiny hand,
The joy that's in a babe's caress,
The soft embrace of happiness,
The sweet good-nights, the shouts of glee
That greet the morning lustily,
Has riches, those who childless live
To know, would all their fortunes give.

Hubbard and Pelletier

Elbert Hubbard of East Aurora was the guest of E. LeRoy Pelletier at luncheon Wednesday.—From the news column.

TWO long-haired friends at table sat
  And sipped some old Sauterne,
  And each one sought throughout the chat
The other's tricks to learn.
"I see some dandruff on your coat,"
  To Elbert whispered Roy;
Said Elbert, clearing out his throat:
  "That's genius, my boy."

"A goodly crop of hair you own,"
  To Roy, then quoth the sage:
"Mine had not quite so bushy grown
  When I was at your age.
I like the way you brush it back,
  'Tis pleasing to the eye,
But one thing I perceive you lack,
  And that's a flowing tie."

"Why wear you such an awful thing?"
  Then questioned Roy the Fra;
"Because it is distinguishing,
  And men know who you are.
The hair and tie have marked me well,"
  In confidence he spake,
"And Elbert Hubbard all can tell
  Where'er my way I take."

Not far from where this famous pair
  Were chatting, sat a crowd:
Said one: "That's Elbert Hubbard there!"
  The voice was fairly loud.
"Which one?" exclaimed another then,
  In still a higher pitch.
"The long-haired one," he said again.
  Said he: "I know, but which?"

The Vote of Thanks

FOR every man who works there are
    A dozen who will let him;
      They'll smiling bask within the shade
    The while his duties fret him.
And when his arduous tasks are done,
    From out the idle ranks
There promptly steps a grateful one
    To move a vote of thanks.

Where more than three foregathered are
    In meeting, club or lodge,
Some cheerful soul must do the work
    That all the others dodge.
Some one for all must toil and plan,
    Some one the money banks,
For which the shirkers to a man
    Will move a vote of thanks.

The many spend their hours in ease,
    While busy are the few;
The glory of the game they want
    But not its work to do.
Untroubled here on earth they live,
    The strength that's in their shanks
They save, to those who toil, to give
    A rising vote of thanks.

Some day when all the work is done
    And rest has settled down,
Perhaps the weary toiler then
    Will wear a golden crown.
Upon his breast may medals flash,
    And at the Heavenly banks
Perhaps they'll even let him cash
    Those rising votes of thanks.

The Sensible Romance of Mildred

MILDRED McGee was a beautiful blond,
　　As fair as peroxide could make her.
　　She was never so shy that a man going by
　　Would imagine that she was a Quaker.
She had suitors that called every night in the week
　　And one of them worked in a shoe shop,
But her "favor-ite" man was a chap named McGann
　　Who was boss of a gang in a glue shop.

Her folks used to scoff at young Patrick McGann
　　For they wished her to marry a plumber;
But Mildred was true to the maker of glue,
　　Though she flirted at times with a drummer.
Though she flirted at times with the pharmacist's
　　　　clerk,
　　And she flirted at times with the baker,
She stuck to McGann, the glue factory man.
　　Not a bit could her fond parents shake her.

"You're in awful bad odor," she said, "with my folks,
　　When you come they both turn up their noses;
But I said when they kicked, that the plumber
　　　　they've picked
　　Isn't scented with attar of roses.
When a girl is in love with a fellow, I've found
　　There's something inside her that rages;
An' I'd rather be true to a sweetheart like you
　　Than a sweet-smelling chap with no wages.

"There's many fine fellows who brag of their jobs
　　An' spend all their coin in a brew shop;
An' take it from me, I'd much rather be
　　The wife of the man in a glue shop.
Not all of us girls can get married to dudes
　　An' college professors an' scholars;
With you I'm content, I'll not stop at a scent
　　So long as you bring in the dollars."

A Good World

IT'S a good old world we're livin' in
    With all its pain an' sorrow;
      A world where friends are givin' in
    To cheer us till tomorrow.
A world where folks come forward, when
    They see our feet are slippin'
To help us till we come again
    To where the honey's drippin'.

I reckon that we'd never know
    How kind an' good our friends are
If trouble's face should never show
    Off yonder where the bends are.
If sudden-like there never came
    A rain to drench a feller
We'd miss the friend who made us claim
    A share of his umbreller.

If never came to us a woe
    That seemed we couldn't bear it,
We'd never positively know
    Which friend would rush to share it.
We'd miss a heap of sweetness, too,
    That we could never borrow,
A sweetness no one ever knew,
    Save it was born of sorrow.

This thought old care has driven in,
    An' grief an' trouble taught me,
It's a good old world we're livin' in
    Despite the woes it's brought me.
For had I never shed a tear,
    Nor known what sorrow's rends are,
I never would have learned down here
    How kind an' good my friends are.

Wisdom's Haunts

'WAY out in the woods there are brothers who read
    By the light of a candle, in Greek,
And in far away places are thousands, indeed,
    Who several languages speak.
I have sat near a stove in a queer little store
    Where the farmers were gathered, and heard
A learned discussion of classical lore
    That my soul with amazement has stirred.

I have looked at rough hands and at storm-weathered
    cheeks
    And imagined their master to be
Uncultured, untutored, as wild as the creeks
    That are rushing their way to the sea;
But I've found just behind the stern mask that he
    wears,
    In the simplest of style and of dress,
A knowledge of life and a grasp of affairs
    That professors don't always possess.

I blush for the arrogant city man's ways
    Who struts in his pomp and his pride,
And thinks that all wisdom in city walls stays,
    And fools in the country abide.
For out in life's forests and out on its plains,
    By the side of her mountains and brooks,
In the roughest of garments are scholars with brains
    Who know the inside of their books.

Oh, fool from the city, who views with a sneer
    What is not of the city itself!
For what are the things that you seem to revere
    But the glint and the glitter of pelf?
You are warped with conceit and are prejudice-blind,
    And you know not the truth of the earth,
That wherever men labor there always you'll find
    The things that are really of worth.

Henry Ford's Offhand Way

Speaking of Henry Ford's purchase of a million dollars' worth of city bonds, Controller Engel said: "He talked about buying those bonds exactly as I would talk about buying a sack of peanuts."—News item.

THERE may be some of us who'd stop and
    scratch our heads awhile
    Before we'd spend a million of our hard-
earned little pile;
And some of us perhaps might want to ponder on the
    deal,
To see the goods before we'd buy, to know that they
    were real,
I'm sure that I should hesitate and count once more
    my hoard
Before I'd write a check like that, but not so Henry
    Ford.
He merely yawned and stretched a bit, and then said:
    "By the way,
A million dollars' worth of bonds, I guess, will do
    today."

And some of us there are who might regret it all our
    lives
If we should do a trick like that and not consult our
    wives.
Before we'd spend a million bones I think we'd hem
    and haw
And then decide to wait a day and put it up to Maw.
I'm sure I shouldn't spend that much upon my own
    accord,
I'd be afraid of what she'd say, but not so Henry Ford.
He just looked through the window at the autumn
    tints of earth
And said: "Those bonds you spoke about. I'll take
    a million's worth."

And some of us, perhaps, before we'd part with such a
    bunch
Would make the salesman take us out and blow us
    off to lunch;

We'd have him bowing down to us and tapping at
    our door,
And make him say a dozen times the things he'd said
    before.
I'm sure before he closed with me and captured his
    reward
I'd make him work a month or two, but not so Henry
    Ford.
He merely said, the while he flicked from off his coat
    a speck:
"Send up a million dollars' worth. I'll write you out
    a check."

Who knows but what he thought about the song
    birds on the farm,
And looked away as though to see the trees in
    autumn's charm?
Perhaps he saw the pumpkins ripe and fodder in the
    shock
And watched a little feller who was driving home
    the stock.
While the agent's heart was beating he was calm as
    he could be,
But perhaps he saw a little boy with patches on his
    knee,
Years and miles away from business, in the town that
    gave him birth,
Who never dreamed he'd buy of bonds a million
    dollars' worth.

The Panama Canal

ABOVE it flies the flag we love,
    Within it is the blood we gave;
    It stands a part and portion of
The courage that once freed the slave.
The strength that fought for liberty
    Hewed out the rock that barred its way;
The men who toiled that it might be
    Were children of the U. S. A.

Within its sides there is no stone
    But what Americans have placed;
Above it other flags have flown
    And seen their labors go to waste.
To build it other lands have tried
    And have deserted in dismay,
But they, who would not be defied,
    Were children of the U. S. A.

Into its massive walls were poured
    The gold that bore the eagle's stamp;
Within each foot of it is stored
    The grit of Valley Forge's camp.
This wedding of divided seas,
    That is a finished fact today,
Stands out among the victories
    That glorify the U. S. A.

No alien land was asked to aid,
    No foreign friend was leaned upon;
This by Americans was made
    While all the world stood looking on.
And molded into every part
    From coast to coast, to last for aye,
There are the blood and flesh and heart
    And genius of the U. S. A.

Beneath Old Glory this was done,
    Beneath Old Glory shall it dwell;
As long as there are seas to run
    This nation's splendor shall it tell.
As long as human hearts shall thrill
    And patriotism men shall sway,
This must remain to speak the skill
    And courage of the U. S. A.

Play the Man

TAKE your troubles
        Best you can.
    Stand right up
    And play the man.

Face 'em just
        As though you knew
You were coming
        Safely through.

Blows will hurt
        And bruise you, maybe,
But don't whimper
        Like a baby.

Stand right up
        And be a man.
Meet your troubles
        Best you can.

The Naughty Little Fellow

WHEN a naughty little fellow stands ashamed in
front of you
And his lips begin to quiver and he's ready to
boo-hoo,
When his big round eyes are filling with the tears he
cannot check,
And at last you find him sobbing with his arms around
your neck,
Don't you get a tender feeling sort of stealing over you,
Till you feel like crying with him?—Well, you bet your
life I do.

When a naughty little fellow, who's the counterpart of
you,
Has been guilty of the very willful deeds you used
to do,
And you've got him on the carpet, where you often
used to stand,
And you quickly feel the pressure of a grimy little
hand
That has stolen rather slyly into yours and thrilled
you through,
Don't you overlook his conduct?—Well, you bet your
life I do.

When a naughty little fellow that has disobeyed his
Ma
Has at last been brought to judgment in the presence
of his Pa,
Who has heard that dreadful story of that very
dreadful day,
And you know that he is worried over what you'll
do or say,
And against your cheek you notice there's a cheek that's
damp and hot,
Are you stern enough to whip him?—Well, you bet
your life I'm not.

The Jedge of Bowie County

(The same being Maclyn Arbuckle.)

HE WAS bo'n way down in Texas, where the
    sun is allus shinin'.
    An' a cloud's so thin it's easy to observe the
      silver linin'.
An' he grew among the quaint folk an' the simple folk
    that labored
In the mint an' melon patches, an' with them for
    years he neighbored;
An' he stored up all the sunshine in the Texas skies
    above him
An' the red hearts of the melons, till they're part an'
    passel of him.

He was Jedge of Bowie county, jedge fer cullud an'
    fer white folk,
Whar he learned the ways of people, learned the
    wrong folk an' the right folk,
An' his heart grew big with kindness fer the ones who
    came with sad things
An' his face grew round with smilin' at the ones who
    came with glad things.
Fer the Jedge of Bowie county all his early days was
    storin'
Up the laughter of old Texas that should set us all
    a-roarin.'

Now the spices of the mint patch an' the juices of
    the melon
Seem to sorter drip an' trickle through the stories
    that he's tellin;
An' he shakes our sides with laughter, and he leads
    us all to gladness,
Till we've plum forgot the troubles that have caused
    us any sadness;
Oh, it seems that life is givin' us an extra joyous
    bounty
When it lets us sit an' listen to the Jedge of Bowie
    County.

Out Fishin'

A FELLER isn't thinkin' mean,
 Out fishin';
 His thoughts are mostly good an' clean,
 Out fishin';
He doesn't knock his fellow men,
Or harbor any grudges then;
A feller's at his finest, when
 Out fishin'.

The rich are comrades to the poor
 Out fishin';
All brothers of a common lure,
 Out fishin';
The urchin with the pin an' string
Can chum with millionaire an' king;
Vain pride is a forgotten thing
 Out fishin'.

A feller gits a chance to dream,
 Out fishin';
He learns the beauties of a·stream,
 Out fishin';
An' he can wash his soul in air
That isn't foul with selfish care,
An' relish plain an' simple fare
 Out fishin'.

A feller has no time fer hate,
 Out fishin';
He isn't eager to be great,
 Out fishin';
He isn't thinkin' thoughts of pelf,
Or goods stacked high upon a shelf,
But he is always just himself,
 Out fishin'.

A feller's glad to be a friend,
 Out fishin';
A helpin' hand he'll always lend,
 Out fishin';

The brotherhood of rod an' line
An' sky an' stream is always fine;
Men come real close to God's design,
Out fishin.'

A feller isn't plotting schemes,
Out fishin';
He's only busy with his dreams,
Out fishin';
His livery is a coat of tan,
His creed: to do the best he can;
A feller's always mostly man,
Out fishin'.

The Toiler

HE swore that he'd be true to her,
If she would only marry him;
That as his wife, throughout his life
She'd never know a moment grim.

He vowed that he would toil for her,
That she should wear the latest things,
He'd robe in furs that form of hers
And deck her hands with diamond rings.

He promised her a motor car,
And maids to answer her commands;
In water hot, with dish and pot
He swore she'd never dip her hands.

Oh, fine the promises he made,
Oh, vows by which her heart was stirred!
And since that time, it's been a crime
The way he's worked to keep his word.

Lonely

THE walls have seemed to say to me
 Where have the sticky fingers gone
That always found their way to me,
 And left their prints to gaze upon.
The halls have worn a gloomy air
 And seemed like tunnels, dark and black,
And it has seemed that every chair
 Has asked me when they're coming back.

The stairs have seemed to speak to me
 Each night as I have climbed alone,
And pitifully squeak to me:
 "Where have the little people flown?"
The beds all smooth and sternly kept
 Have said with faces drawn and white
Where are the curly heads that slept
 On us, so sweetly, every night?

The untouched toys have stared at me
 As if to say the days are long,
And all their dolls have glared at me
 As though accusing me of wrong.
And every rug so straight and stiff
 Has seemed to sigh for rumpling feet,
And worn a sorry look as if
 It missed the mud-tracks of the street.

The bird has twittered low to me
 A sort of solemn, sad refrain
As though he tried to show to me
 He wishes they were near again.
But soon the walls and halls and chairs
 Will know once more the charm they lack,
And little feet will race the stairs,
 They've sent me word they're coming back.

Arcady

WHERE is the road to Arcady,
   Where is the path that leads to peace,
Where shall I find the bliss to be,
   Where shall the weary wanderings cease?
These are the questions that come to me,
Where is the road to Arcady?

Is there a mystic time and place
   To which some day shall the traveler fare,
Where there is never a frowning face
   And never a burden hard to bear,
Where we as children shall romp and race?
Is there a mystic time and place?

For Arcady is an earthly sphere
   Where only the gentlest breezes blow,
A port of rest for the weary here,
   Where the velvet grass and the clover grow.
I question it oft, is it far or near?
For Arcady is an earthly sphere.

And the answer comes: it is very near,
   It's there at the end of a little street,
Where your children's voices are ringing clear
   And you catch the patter of little feet.
Where is the spot that is never drear?
And the answer comes: it is very near.

For each man buildeth his Arcady,
   And each man fashions his Port of Rest;
And never shall earth spot brighter be
   Than the little home that with peace is blessed.
So seek it not o'er the land and sea,
For each man buildeth his Arcady.

The Old-Fashioned Parents

THE good old-fashioned mothers and the good
old-fashioned dads
With their good old-fashioned lassies and their
good old-fashioned lads,
Still walk the lanes of loving in their simple, tender
ways
As they used to do back yonder in the good old-
fashioned days.

They dwell in every city and they live in every town,
Contentedly and happy and not hungry for renown;
On every street you'll find 'em in their simple gar-
ments clad,
The good old-fashioned mother and the good old-
fashioned dad.

There are some who sigh for riches, there are some who
yearn for fame,
And a few misguided people who no longer blush at
shame;
But the world is full of mothers and the world is full of
dads
Who are making sacrifices for their little girls and lads.

They are growing old together, arm in arm they walk
along,
And their hearts with love are beating and their voices
sweet with song;
They still share their disappointments and they share
their pleasures, too,
And whatever be their fortune, to each other they are
true.

They are watching at the bedside of a baby pale and
white,
And they kneel and pray together for the care of God
at night;

They are romping with their children in the fields of
    clover sweet,
And devotedly they guard them from the perils of the
    street.

They are here in countless numbers, just as they have
    always been,
And their glory is untainted by the selfish and the
    mean.
And I'd hate to still be living, it would dismal be and
    sad,
If we'd no old-fashioned mother and we'd no old-
    fashioned dad.

A Prayer

IF I am to suffer pain,
    Let me bear it as a man.
    If I'm not the hights to gain
Let me do the best I can.
Let me travel on my way
    Glad of heart and with a smile,
Finding something every day
    That is really worth the while.

If I am to reach my goal
    Let me not grow proud and vain,
Without arrogance of soul
    Let me victories attain.
Let me travel on my way
    Winning whatsoe'er I can
But remembering every day
    What I owe my fellow man.

He Earned His Way

HE rose unto the hights of fame
    And with the great men stood,
    He heard the people cheer his name
And speak of him as good.
Success at last he had attained
    By toiling day by day;
His father's name was unprofaned,
His crest of honor was unstained,
    He earned his way.

He had not sought the easy road
    Nor tried a doubtful scheme,
But he had borne his heavy load
    Up hill and over stream.
He had not stooped to do a wrong
    That might not be unlearned;
But though the way at times seemed long
He plodded on with courage strong
    And every victory earned.

He heard men whisper in the night,
    That venturing disgrace,
And stepping from the path of right
    But hiding every trace,
Were all he had to do to win,
    That honor could be feigned,
But still he kept a lifted chin,
Filled with the holy thought within,
    To earn whate'er he gained.

He rose unto the hights of fame,
    And with the great men stood;
He never compromised with shame,
    Nor bartered what was good.
With head erect he toiled along,
    With clean hands for the fray,
He heard the gossip of the throng
That many profited by wrong,
    But earned his way.

The Toy-Strewn Home

GIVE me the house where the toys are strewn,
    Where the dolls are asleep in the chairs,
    Where the building blocks and the toy bal-
        loon
And the soldiers guard the stairs;
Let me step in a house where the tiny cart
    With the horses rules the floor,
And rest comes into my weary heart
    For I am at home once more.

Give me the house with the toys about,
    With the battered old train of cars,
The box of paints and the books left out,
    And the ship with her broken spars;
Let me step in a house at the close of day
    That is littered with children's toys,
And dwell once more in the haunts of play
    With the echoes of by-gone noise.

Give me the house where the toys are seen,
    The house where the children romp,
And I'll happier be than man has been
    'Neath the gilded dome of pomp.
Let me see the litter of bright-eyed play
    Strewn over the parlor floor,
And the joys I knew in a far-off day
    Will gladden my heart once more.

Whoever has lived in a toy-strewn home,
    Though feeble he be and gray,
Will yearn, no matter how far he roam,
    For the glorious disarray
Of the little home with its littered floor
    That was his in the by-gone days,
And his heart will throb as it throbbed before,
    When he rests where a baby plays.

Snooping 'Round

LAST night I caught him on his knees and
looking underneath the bed,
And oh, the guilty look he wore, and oh, the
stammered words he said,
When I, pretending to be cross, said: "Hey, young
fellow, what's your game?"
As if, back in the long ago, I hadn't also played the
same;
As if, upon my hands and knees, I hadn't many a
time been found
When, thinking of the Christmas Day, I'd gone up-
stairs to snoop around.

But there he stood and hung his head; the rascal
knew it wasn't fair.
"I jes' was wonderin', he said, "jes' what it was that's
under there,
It's somepin' all wrapped up an' I thought mebbe it
wuz a sled,
Becoz I saw a piece of wood 'at's stickin' out all
painted red."
"If mother knew," I said to him, "you'd get a licking
I'll be bound,
But just clear out of here at once, and don't you ever
snoop around."

And as he scampered down the stairs, I stood and
chuckled to myself
As I remembered how I'd oft explored the topmost
closet shelf.
It all came back again to me with what a shrewd and
cunning way
I, too, had often sought to solve the mysteries of
Christmas Day.
How many times my daddy, too, had come upstairs
without a sound
And caught me, just as I'd begun my clever scheme
to snoop around.

And oh, I envied him his plight, I envied him the joy
    he feels
Who knows that every drawer that's locked some
    treasure dear to him conceals;
I envied him his Christmas fun and wished that it
    again were mine
To seek to solve the mysteries by paper wrapped and
    bound by twine.
Some day he'll come to understand that all the time
    I stood and frowned,
I saw a boy of years ago who also used to snoop
    around.

Life

LIFE has its ups and downs, of course,
    Its happy marriage and divorce,
    It has its joys, it has its woes,
It has its ayes, it has its noes,
It has its ins and outs, that's plain,
Its sunshine and its days of rain,
It has its good points and its bad,
Its cheerful moments and its sad;
Its births and deaths, its smiles and tears,
Its faiths and doubts, its hopes and fears,
And looked at, too, from every phase,
It has death beaten forty ways.

Fixing the Shame

THEY put him in jail for the thing he'd done,
    For that was the law they'd made;
      They turned the key on his youth till he
    The price of his crime had paid.
And the wise judge said as he sentenced him,
    And spoke from the facts he knew:
"The deed was yours, and the wide outdoors
    No longer belongs to you."

Oh, it isn't so long ago there went
    A toddling lad of three
At the close of day for a bit of play
    Astride of his father's knee.
And the father scowled and sent him off.
    "Go play with the lads outside,
Don't bother me with your pranks," said he;
    And he sneered when the youngster cried.

And the father went to his work all day
    And went to his bed at night,
And he gave no heed to the baby's need
    Nor shared in the lad's delight.
He never knew who his playmates were,
    Nor followed him off to school,
But in manner grim he punished him
    Whenever he broke the rule.

Midnight came not so long ago
    And the youngster was not in bed,
But the father slept while the mother kept
    The watch that all mothers dread.
And whenever the mother spoke of him
    Through the long black hours of night,
As the cold wind howled the father growled:
    "Don't worry, the boy's all right."

Society said at the end of things!
    "The doer of crime must pay;
In a grated cell we'll make him dwell,
    Shut in from the light of day."

But I like to think that the Judge on High
Who rights all our earthly wrongs
At another time, will fix that crime
Exactly where it belongs.

Service

To the cause one man gave gold,
    Then withdrew into his den
From the battle line, and told
How he served his fellowmen.

When they came and begged for aid,
    Gladly from his purse he gave,
And he hoped that those he paid
    Would continue being brave.

"To the cause," another said,
    "I've no gold that I can give,
But I'll fight for it instead,
    Just so long as I shall live."

Day by day and night by night,
    He that hath no gold to spare,
In the thickest of the fight
    Fought and cheered his fellows there.

There are hundreds here to share,
    For the principle, their pelf,
But he better serves who'll dare
    To a cause to give himself.

This world does not need your coin
    Half so much as it needs you,
What it wants is men to join
    In the work it has to do.

Off to School

IT doesn't seem a year ago that I was tumbling out of bed,
    The icy steps that lead below at 1 a. m., barefoot, to tread,
And puttering round the kitchen stove, while chills ran up and down my form
As I stood there and waited for her bottled dinner to get warm;
Then sampled it to see that it was not too hot or not too cool,
That doesn't seem a year ago, and now she's trudging off to school.

It doesn't seem a month ago that I was teaching her to walk,
And holding out my arms to her.   And that was 'fore she learned to talk.
I stood her up against the wall, eager, yet watchful lest she fall,
Then suddenly she came to me—the first two steps those feet so small
Had, unassisted, ever made!   Those feet I hope to guide and rule;
That doesn't seem a month ago—and now she's trudging off to school.

It doesn't seem a week ago that we were playing peek-a-boo,
She'd lift her little dress and hide her face as all the babies do;
And then we'd laugh and romp and shout, and I would ride her pig-a-back.
A pair of gay disturbers we, with not a care along life's track!
The days were meant for laughter then, and I was glad to play the fool,
That doesn't seem a week ago—and now she's trudging off to school.

Oh, Father Time, line deep my brow, and tinge my
thinning hair with gray,
Deal harshly with my battered form as you go speed-
ing on your way;
Print on my face your marks of years, and stamp me
with your yesterdays,
But, oh, tread softly now, I pray, the ground whereon
my baby plays.
Pass over her with gentle touch; to keep her young
break every rule,
But yesterday she was a babe—and now she's trudging
off to school.

Human Failings

I RECKON when our days are done
And God takes up our record sheets,
And sees the battles we have won,
He'll want to read of our defeats.

Our little failings He will view,
And gaze at us with kindly smile,
And maybe say: "I see that you
Have faltered every little while."

I reckon that he'll like to see
The blots and blemishes between
The splendid works of you and me,
To learn how human we have been.

His Rattle He Throws on the Floor

WHEN something or other has made him feel
    glad,
    His rattle he throws on the floor;
The times he is good and the times he is bad,
    His rattle he throws on the floor.
When there is a smile on his pink little face,
Or a pin that is holding his garments in place
Has slipped from its moorings, he makes a grimace
    And his rattle he throws on the floor.

When we are alone for the meal we call tea,
    His rattle he throws on the floor;
And on the occasions we have company,
    His rattle he throws on the floor.
When the cat strokes her side on the leg of his chair,
When no one is looking, or when we all stare,
When he's tired, or he isn't, of sitting up there,
    His rattle he throws on the floor.

When he thinks that he ought to have something to eat
    His rattle he throws on the floor;
When he's eaten too much—his most usual feat—
    His rattle he throws on the floor.
When he's hot, when he's cold, when he's bold, when
    he's shy,
When he's thinking of starting or stopping a cry,
Before waving "how-do" to his dad, or "good-bye,"
    His rattle he throws on the floor.

And his mother does nothing but wait on him when
    His rattle he throws on the floor;
She recovers it for him, but straightway again
    His rattle he throws on the floor.
Out of patience, we once on the floor let it stay,
But he put up a howl, for he wanted to play,
So relenting, we gave it to him, and straightway
    His rattle he threw on the floor.

Sacrifices

BEHIND full many a gift there lies
　　A splendid tale of sacrifice.

On Christmas morn a mother's hand
　　About a young girl's neck will place
A trinket small, and she will stand
　　With radiant smiles upon her face
To see her daughter decked in gold,
　　Nor will she think, nor will she care
That she may suffer from the cold
　　Because that bauble glistens there.

A child will wake on Christmas Day
　　And find his stocking filled with toys;
The home will ring with laughter gay,
　　That boy be glad as richer boys.
And there a mother fond will sing
　　A song of joy to hear his shout,
Forgetting every needed thing
　　That she will have to do without.

A heart that's brimming o'er with love
　　Will suffer gladly for a friend,
And take no time in thinking of
　　How much it can afford to spend.
And suddenly on Christmas morn
　　Will gladness beam from shining eyes,
A gladness that alone was born
　　Of someone's willing sacrifice.

Let cynics scoff howe'er they will
　　And say but fools such presents give,
There'll be such sacrifices till
　　All human love shall cease to live.
'Twould be a dreary world of thrift,
　　Of barren ways, and sunless skies,
If no one ever gave a gift
　　That was not born of sacrifice.

The brightest gifts that us reward
Are those the givers can't afford.

89

Tuckered Out

YOU don't weigh more than thirty pounds,
　　Your legs are little, plump and fat,
　　And yet you patter on your rounds
The whole day long within our flat.
Yes, ceaselessly, you come and go,
　　In search of things you want to see,
You're only two years old, but oh
　　You walk the strength right out of me.

A dozen times a day or more
　　You gayly lead me up the stairs,
Then back to try the kitchen door,
　　Then round about the parlor chairs.
You come and take me by the hand
　　And splendidly you march away
Until by night I scarce can stand,
　　While you are fresh and keen for play.

You know not what it is to tire,
　　You never seem to care for rest;
You seem to have but one desire
　　And that's to go, 'till you're undressed.
And this tonight I'll say to you
　　As you are tugging at my knee,
That it is all that I can do
　　To keep the pace you set for me.

Oh, little chap, with tireless step,
　　Oh, little laughing chap of two,
I somehow wish I had your "pep"
　　And could keep up as well as you!
I wish I had what you possess,
　　The strength to romp and play and run,
Yet every Sunday, I confess,
　　I'm tuckered out when night comes on.

Memories of Tomorrow

THESE are the memories of tomorrow,
  Smile of friend we meet today,
  Sympathy to soothe our sorrow,
  Roses blooming by the way;
Little jests to cheer the living,
  Little deeds of kindness done,
Thought to them shall we be giving
  When the years have wandered on.

What seems slight to us at present
  Will grow big in other days;
Memory will make it pleasant,
  We'll retread these happy ways.
We shall sigh to greet the brother
  That today we hurry by;
Joys we share with one another
  We'll remember, you and I.

Little pranks that we are playing,
  Little songs that now we sing,
Orchard lanes that we are straying
  Will come back, and with them bring
Far more gladness, far more sweetness
  Than we seem to find today,
We shall see them in completeness
  When the present slips away.

Gentle skies that float above us,
  Babies romping 'round the floor,
Friends who show us that they love us,
  Roses blooming at the door;
Hours now dark with care and sorrow,
  Love that comes to dry the eye
Are the memories of tomorrow
  We shall treasure, you and I.

Tinkerin' at Home

SOME folks there be that seems to need
    excitement fast an' furious.
    An' reckon all the joys that have no thrill in
      'em are spurious.
Some think that pleasure's only found down where
    the lights are shining
An' where an orchestra's at work the while the folks
    are dining.
Still others seek it at their play, while some there are
    who roam,
But I am happiest when I am tinkerin' 'round the
    home.

I like to wear my oldest clothes, an' fuss around the
    yard
An' dig a flower bed now an' then, and pensively
    regard
The mornin' glories climbin' all along the wooden
    fence,
An' do the little odds an' ends that aren't of
    consequence.
I like to trim the hedges, an' touch up the paint a bit,
An' sort of take a homely pride in keepin' all things fit.
An' I don't envy rich folks who are sailin' o'er the foam
When I can spend a day or two in tinkerin' 'round the
    home.

If I were fixed with money, as some other people are,
I'd take things mighty easy. I'd not travel very far.
I'd jes' wear my oldest trousers an' my flannel shirt,
    an' stay
An' guard my vine an' fig tree in an old man's tender
    way.
I'd bathe my soul in sunshine every mornin', an' I'd
    bend
My back to pick the roses. Oh, I'd be a watchful
    friend

To everything around the place, an' in the twilight
    gloam
I'd thank the Lord for lettin' me jes' tinker 'round the
    home.

But since I've got to hustle in the turmoil of the town,
An' don't expect I'll ever be allowed to settle down
An' live among the roses an' the tulips an' the phlox,
Or spend my time in carin' for the noddin' hollyhocks,
I've come to the conclusion that perhaps in Heaven I
    may
Get a chance to know the pleasures that I'm yearnin'
    for today;
An' I'm goin' to ask the good Lord, when I've climbed
    the golden stair,
If he'll kindly let me tinker 'round the home we've got
    up there.

Not Crossing Bridges

MEBBE I shall weep tomorrow,
    Mebbe I shall lose my job,
    Mebbe bowed in grief and sorrow
I shall sit alone and sob.

Mebbe trouble grim is comin',
    Mebbe care is on the way,
Mebbe I'll be busy glummin'
    Over things some other day.

Mebbe foes will come assailin'
    An' at last I'll have to quit;
But before I start to wailin'
    I shall wait until I'm hit.

Little Marie

I REMEMBER the day that you came to me,
  Little Marie,
  The nurse brought you out so that I might
   see
   Little Marie.
Oh, this heart o' mine leapt as I gazed at you
And got my first peep at those eyes o' blue,
And I kissed your cheek and I hugged you, too,
   Little Marie.

I remember the very first word you spake,
   Little Marie,
The very first steps that you tried to take,
   Little Marie;
I remember the very first bump you got
And you came to me and I kissed the spot;
Of your bumps and bruises I've cured a lot,
   Little Marie.

The birds in the tree still sing your name,
   Little Marie;
The roses somehow aren't quite the same,
   Little Marie;
And there isn't a nook in the home or yard
But what like my battered old heart you've scarred;
And we miss you so, and it's oh, so hard!
   Little Marie.

You smiled when I said I was losing you,
   Little Marie;
You said you'd come back in a year or two,
   Little Marie;
And your mother prays, and I say amen,
That we'll be grandpa and grandma then,
And you will place in our arms again
   A little Marie.

Father's Chore

MY Pa can hit his thumb nail with a hammer and keep still,
    He can cut himself while shaving an' not swear;
If a ladder slips beneath him an' he gets a nasty spill
    He can smile as though he really didn't care.
But the pan beneath the ice box—when he goes to empty that—
    Then a sound-proof room the children have to hunt,
For we have a sad few minutes in our very pleasant flat
    When the water in it splashes down his front.

My Pa believes his temper should be all the time controlled,
    He doesn't rave at every little thing,
When his collar-button underneath the chiffonier has rolled
    A snatch of merry ragtime he will sing.
But the pan beneath the ice box—when to empty that he goes—
    As he stoops to drag it out we hear a grunt,
From the kitchen comes a rumble, an' then everybody knows
    That he's splashed the water in it down his front.

Now the distance from the ice box to the sink's not very far,
    I'm sure it isn't over twenty feet,
But though very short the journey, it is long enough for Pa
    As he travels it disaster grim to meet.
And it's seldom that he makes it without accident, although
    In the summer time it is his nightly stunt;
And he says a lot of language that no gentleman should know
    When the water in it splashes down his front.

Real Lessons

THESE are the lessons I would learn,
    Not how to climb above all men,
    Not how the greatest sums to earn,
    Not how to wield a master pen;
But I would learn how I can be
    A little kinder than before,
How I can live more patiently
    And help my friends a little more.

And I would learn to better show
    My gratitude for favors had,
To see more of the good below
    And less of what I think is bad.
To live not always in the day
    To come, and count the joys to be,
But to remember, as I stray,
    The past and what it brought to me.

To judge my life, not from today,
    Nor what tomorrow it may mean,
But from each footstep of the way
    And from each pleasure that has been,
Remembering in each present woe
    The love and laughter I have known;
And to be grateful as I go,
    For joys that once I called my own.

These are lessons I would learn:
    To be as brave in grief and care
As I am when it is my turn
    To tread the road where all is fair.
More grateful I would learn to be
    For what has been, as on I tread,
And to press forward cheerfully.
    Content to face what lies ahead.

One-Sided Faith

I KNOW the rose will bloom again
  As soon as it is June,
The robin will return by then
  To sing his merry tune.
I know the wintry cold will pass,
  The gray clouds change to blue,
But I think my present woe, alas!
  Must last my whole life through.

I view my little garden bare
  And smile from day to day,
I know the green will glisten there
  As soon as it is May.
I face the winter, brave of heart,
  I know that it will go,
But every little ache and smart
  Sets me to grieving so.

If I can view the winter's snow,
  My garden desolate
And smile, because right well I know
  If I will only wait
The days of spring will soon return,
  And bring me back the rose,
Have I not wit enough to learn
  That time will cure my woes?

The Thumbed Collar

"GO up and change your collar," mother often
    says to me,
        "For you can't go out in that one, it's as
dirty as can be.
There are splotches on the surface where they very
    plainly show."
"That is very queer," I answer, "it was clean an
    hour ago."
But I guess just what has happened, and in this it's
    clearly summed:
He who lets a baby love him often gets his collar
    thumbed.

I've been dressed up for a dinner, in a shirt of snowy
    white,
And I've stooped to kiss the rascal, and his arms have
    held me tight;
I have clasped him to my bosom as he gooed and
    gurgled, then
I have found it necessary that I change my shirt
    again.
For the snowy, spotless surface, with some sticky
    sweet was gummed.
He who lets a baby love him often gets his linen
    thumbed.

I have gone downtown o' mornings thinking I was
    clean and neat,
And have had some kind friend stop me as I walked
    along the street
With the startling information that I wore a collar
    soiled,
As he saw the prints and traces where those little
    thumbs had toiled;
And I've made this explanation—it's a song I long
    have hummed—
He who loves a little baby often get his collar
    thumbed.

And I'm rather proud I reckon, to have people here
    allude
To the prints upon my collars; they're my badge of
    servitude.
They're the proudest marks I carry, and I really
    dread the day
When there'll be no sticky fingers, when I start to go
    away,
To reach up and soil my neckwear; and my heart
    sometimes is numbed
When I think the day is coming when my collars
    won't be thumbed.

Fame

FAME is a fickle jade at best,
    And he who seeks to win her smile
    Must trudge, disdaining play or rest,
O'er many a long and weary mile.

Nor must he work alone for her,
    Nor labor only for her cheers,
For doing this, it may occur
    That he shall only reap her sneers.

But when he's ceased to care for self,
    And is content to work and wait
For something better far than pelf,
    Fame welcomes him among the great.

Envy

GIVE me a little girl of three,
    A boy of four or five,
      And you can bet that I will be
The gladdest man alive.
I envy no rich man his gold,
    Or motor car that skids,
But green with envy I behold
    The poor man's bunch of kids.

Give me a boy of eight or nine,
    A girl of six or seven
And I would count this world as fine
    And very close to Heaven.
I envy no man's fame today,
    For that I make no bids,
But envying, I go my way,
    The poor man's bunch of kids.

With such a troop to follow me
    And romp about my feet,
To climb at night upon my knee,
    I'd count life's struggle sweet.
I envy none who's trouble free,
    But till death shuts my lids
With envy I shall always see
    The poor man's bunch of kids.

Memorial Day

THERE are new graves for our roses
  In God's acres where we stand,
  And each passing year discloses
  Thinner ranks in each command.
There are eyes still red with weeping,
  There are heart aches that are new
For the absent heroes keeping
  Step with God's command in blue.

Eyes that saw the smoke of battle
  Now are closing every day;
Ears that heard the muskets rattle
  Now are deaf to all we say.
Lips that used to tell the story
  Have been silenced, and we strew
On their graves the blooms of glory,
  Roses drenched with love and dew.

From the earthly ranks they're falling,
  Snow-crowned heroes, one by one;
'Tis the Great Commander calling,
  And their souls are marching on.
And the day is swiftly coming
  When our heroes all will march
To the sound of angel drumming,
  Under God's triumphal arch.

They are going, quickly going,
  To the heavenly camps above,
But each rose today is showing
  They will always live in love.
And where liberty is treasured
  And the flag of freedom waves,
With a love that is unmeasured
  Men will decorate their graves.

Warning the Carpenter

SAY, Mister Carpenter, you know, you got me
  spanked last night,
    I guess your Pa and Ma forgot to teach you
      what was right;
An' I can't come here any more to watch you build
  that fence,
Coz my Pa says a man like you ain't got a bit of sense.
You 'member yesterday, when you was nailing up a
  board
An' hit your thumb an awful whack the drefful things
  you swored,
Well, I felt sorry for you then, coz I am only three,
An' I supposed 'at what you said would be all right
  for me.

Las' night I was a-playin' wif my hammer an' a box
An' hit my thumb jus' like you did two terrible hard
  knocks;
My Ma an' Pa were standing near, an' bofe of 'em
  turned red
When I let loose an' said out loud the drefful things
  you said.
You never told me it was wrong; it seemed to comfort
  you,
An' when I hit my thumb I s'posed it was all right
  to do.
But you will never get to be an angel when you die
Becoz you used such wicked words an' let your temper
  fly.

My Pa, he took me on his knee an' spanked me for
  it, too,
An' Ma, she jus' sat down an' cried the whole long
  evenin' through;
She says there ought to be a law to keep bad men away
From decent neighborhoods like ours where little
  children play.
You let me get a wallopin'. An' I don't think it fair,
Say! Ain't you got no Pa an' Ma to teach you not to
  swear?

It's all your fault that I got licked, an' Ma says when
    you die
There ain't a-goin' to be no place for you up in the sky;
An' Pa says 'at you ought to know 'at little fellow's
    ears
Pick up the things that bad men say. An' if he ever
    hears
That I've been hangin' round this place he don't know
    what he'll do;
I guess he'll tell your Pa an' Ma, an' you'll get
    walloped, too.

A Song

ROUGH be the road and long,
    Steep be the hills ahead,
    Grant that my faith be strong,
    Fearlessly let me tread.
After the day's hard test
Home—with its peaceful rest.

Heavy my burdens be,
    Let me not falter though,
Soon I shall come to see
    Home, where the roses grow.
Home, where the swallows nest,
Home, with its peaceful rest.

This grant to me at last,
    When I have ceased to roam,
When all my cares are past,
    I may be welcomed home,
Home, where is none distressed,
Home, with its peaceful rest.

The First Rule of Golf

(In which Ye Ed attempts the millionaire's game and obeys the first rule of golf, which is to put back the turf.)

WE stood at the tee and the driver we swung,
      Then we put back the turf;
  At the ball, then a thing called the
      "mashie," we flung,
      Then we put back the turf.
"There's a fine mid-iron shot I am sure you can do,"
Said a friend, "you should get on the green then in
      two;"
We tried it, then painted the atmosphere blue
      And put back the turf.

We tried for a shot o'er a bunker ahead,
      Then we put back the turf;
We attempted to loft, but the ball remained dead,
      Then we put back the turf.
We tackled the niblick, the putter, the cleek,
They went through the air with a whistle and shriek,
And our manner was humble and abject and meek
      As we put back the turf.

We posed, a la Travers, and let the club go,
      Then we put back the turf;
The pellet was nicely addressed for a blow,
      Then we put back the turf;
Out there on the links with the sun shining warm
To watch us the spectators came in a swarm,
And they freely remarked on our wonderful form
      As we put back the turf.

At the first, second, third, fourth and fifth holes men
  see
      Where we put back the turf;
From the fifth to the ninth it's as plain as can be
      Where we put back the turf.
And we answered when asked, as we sat at a meal,
Our honest opinion of golf to reveal:
"It's great, but it's terribly hard on the heel
      When you put back the turf."

'Erbert's H'opinion

'IF a Yankee cutthroat 'acks 'is poor h'old
      mother,
    H'it tykes a year to pack 'im h'off to jyle;
'E can h'always dig h'up some h'excuse or h'other
    To keep your justice creepin' like a snyle.
But h'in H'England, h'if a bloke gets h'into trouble,
    To the pen h'in 'arf a jiffy 'e will roam;
H'if 'e mykes a fight 'is punishment will double,
    We do things so much better h'over 'ome.

H'if a bloomin' Yankee starts to build a dwelling
    'E slaps h'it h'up without a bit h'of care,
In 'arf the time h'it tykes me in the telling,
    'E 'as the chimney pot h'up in the h'air.
But h'in H'England 'ouses h'always larst forever,
    We build 'em right, from cellar h'up to dome;
H'although you bloomin' Yankees think you're
      clever,
    We do things so much better h'over 'ome.

'Ere h'its always 'elter-skelter, rush and bustle,
    H'and h'its pell-mell h'into h'everything you ·
      do;
You h'even teach your children 'ow to 'ustle
    Your meals you never tyke the time to chew.
But h'in H'England, when h'it's tea time, we stop
      working,
H'an, H'I wish that H'I was back h'across the
      foam,
H'in me 'ead the notion still h'is plynely lurking,
    We do things so much better h'over 'ome.

The Fun of Forgiving

SOMETIMES I'm almost glad to hear when I
get home that they've been bad,
And though I try to look severe, within my
heart I'm really glad
When mother sadly tells to me the list of awful things
they've done,
Because when they come tearfully, forgiving them is
so much fun.

I like to have them all alone, with no one near to hear
or see,
Then as their little faults they own, I like to take them
on my knee
And talk it over and pretend the whipping soon must
be begun;
And then to kiss them at the end—forgiving them is so
much fun.

Within the world there's no such charms, as children
penitent and sad,
Who put two soft and chubby arms around your neck
when they've been bad.
And as you view their trembling lips, away your
temper starts to run,
And from your mind all anger slips—forgiving them
is so much fun.

If there were nothing to forgive, I wonder if we'd love
them so,
If they were wise enough to live as grown-ups do, and
ever go
Along the pleasant path of right, with ne'er a fault
from sun to sun,
A lot of joys we'd miss at night—forgiving them is so
much fun.

A Choice

RATHER win a brother's smile
    Than a stack of dollar notes,
      Rather do one thing worth while
    Than have all the nation's votes;
Rather tread the simple way
    Where the sweet wild roses are
Than to dress in glad array
    And be prince or king or czar.

Somehow, when I sum it up,
    I would rather be a friend
Than by force snatch vict'ry's cup
    And be hated in the end.
I would rather leave behind
    Tender gentle thoughts of me
Than have those who follow find
    Stains upon my memory.

Rather do the simple things,
    Rather play a lowly part
Than to win the praise of kings
    And be cold and hard of heart.
I would rather fail to be
    Rich or famous on the earth,
Rather dwell in poverty
    If my deeds will tell my worth.

Rather feel a brother's hand
    Clasped in mine, as friendship's vow
Than in pomp and pride to stand
    With a crown upon my brow.
Rather have one find me true
    Than have thousands call me great
And despise the things I do,
    Turning from me in their hate.

The Value of a Telephone

ꓡAST night we had a hurry call to go to daughter
  May,
  Her husband said that Ma and me were
   wanted right away,
An' so, though it was after 12, an' bitter cold outside,
We hustled out of bed an' dressed an' took a trolley
  ride;
An' Jim—that is her husband—met us with a gracious
  bow
An' said to me as we stepped in: "Well, you're a
  grandpa now."

An' Ma went flyin' up the stairs, an' Jim an' I stayed
  down,
An' talked about the great event, Jim in his dressin'
  gown,
As comfortable as you please. An' then he sorter
  smiled
An' said: "An hour or two ago I thought that I'd
  go wild,
The stork was hoverin' above, an' I was all alone,
I'll tell you, Dad, I burned the wires of that old
  telephone.

"I telephoned the doctor an' I telephoned the nurse,
  An' I'm sure the sort of service that I got could not
   be worse;
  I telephoned the druggist, an' I 'phoned the neigh-
   bors, too,
  An' then when I was through with them, I telephoned
   to you.
  Each minute seemed an hour to me; I thought they'd
   never come,
  You bet I was a busy boy. I made the old wires hum."

An' then I laughed an' said to him: "Why, when
  your wife was born,
We didn't have a telephone the neighbors 'round to
  warn;

They got me out of bed at 1 a. m. an' said to me:
'You'd better get the doctor now, an' get him here
    at 3.'
I had to run four miles that night to bang upon his
    door,
An' then to get the nurse I had to hike about two
    more.

"That isn't all the hikin' that the women made me do;
I had to get her mother's folks—the same as she made
    you;
There were no trolley cars back then, at least that
    late at night;
I ran four stitches in my side, and finished ten pounds
    light;
I walked an' did a double trot, a gallop and a pace,
An' I didn't even stop to wipe the sweat beads from
    my face.

"An' here you're in your dressin' gown, an' sittin' by
    the fire,
An' everybody's on the job, all summoned by the
    wire.
You haven't even left your house or felt the winter's
    chill—
Just think, my boy, without a 'phone, why, you'd be
    running still!
You'd still be hiking somewhere an' wearing out your
    shoes,
An' pausin' for your second wind—that's how I
    spread the news!"

The Sympathetic Minister

MY father is a peaceful man,
        He tries in every way he can
        To live a life of gentleness
And patience all the while;
He says that needless fretting's vain,
That it's absurd to be profane,
That nearly every wrong can be
Adjusted with a smile.
Yet try no matter how he will,
There's one thing that annoys him still,
One thing that robs him of his calm
And makes him very sore;
He cannot keep his self-control
When with a shovel full of coal
He misses where it's headed for,
And hits the furnace door.

He measures with a careful eye,
The space for which he's soon to try,
Then grabs his trusty shovel up
And loads it in the bin,
Then turns and with a healthy lunge,
That's two parts swing and two parts plunge
He lets go at the furnace fire,
Convinced it will go in!
And then we hear a sudden smack,
The cellar air turns blue and black;
Above the rattle of the coal
We hear his awful roar.
From dreadful language upward hissed
We know that father's aim has missed
And that his shovel full of coal
Went up against the door.

The minister was here one day
For supper, and Pa went away
To fix the furnace fire, and soon
We heard that awful roar.

And through the furnace pipes there came
Hot words that made Ma blush for shame,
"It strikes me," said the minister,
"He hit the furnace door."
    Ma turned away and hung her head,
"I'm so ashamed," was all she said;
And then the minister replied:
"Don't worry. I admit
That when I hit the furnace door
And spill the coal upon the floor,
I quite forget the cloth I wear
—er—swear a little bit."

Hope ·

HOPE sings of tomorrow,
        When trouble rules today;
    Bowed down tonight in sorrow
The morning may be gay.

Hope looks forward ever
        And sings of joys to be,
For trouble's grip is never
        On us eternally.

Today though trouble lingers
        And every hour is glum,
Hope points with rosy fingers
        To joys that are to come.

Friends

MOST every day
    I find my way
      Made smoother,
Brighter, by a friend;
Some kindly word
My heart has stirred
And caused my
Spirits to ascend.

A handclasp here,
A smile sincere,
A kindly deed
In friendship done
Have made me feel
That life is real
And I have gladly
Journeyed on.

Where'er I turn
'Tis but to learn
The sweetness of
The heart of man,
For everywhere
Are friends, I swear,
Who smooth my path
Where'er they can.

There is no day
Howe'er so gray
But what some friend
With cheerful voice
Is glad to share
My bit of care
And give me
Reason to rejoice.

Welcoming the New Year

At 10 p. m.

COME, let us make merry with innocent mirth,
Let us drink to the year that is dying;
Let us wish one another the best that's on
earth,
Now quickly, the moments are flying.
Here waiter! Come, fill up the glasses again,
Tonight we are here to be merry,
Forgot are the grief and the trouble and pain ·
That the old fellow brought in his ferry.
Nothing boisterous here, as we chat and we drink
At the table we've rented for folly,
But in friendship this evening our glasses we clink,
To welcome the year and be jolly.

At 11 p. m.

Some old-fashioned folks stay at home to be gay
Where ther'sh never an orchestra playing,
But I like the thrill of a modern cafe,
I believe in all customs obeying.
Then here's to ush all at the table tonight,
May the New Year bring nothing but gladness,
And cheeks that are rosy and eyes that are bright,
And may we know none of its badness.
Now, waiter, just fill up thoshe glasses again,
May you never know sad melancholy,
May the year that is coming bring you little rain,
May you always succeed and be jolly.

At 12 m.

Ish a Happy New Year! May you alwaysh be gay!
Whoopee! for zhe New Year (hic) arriving;
Do youshe fellersh know what I'm trying to sha?
Do youshe get (hic) at what I am driving?
Ish all right now fellersh, lesh fill up zhe glass,
(Hic) I like yesh and I want t' show it.
Yesh mighty fine fellersh. (Hic) Yesh all first class
And I want zhe New Year to know it.
Hersh a happy New Year. Whoopee for yesh all!
May yesh never go wrong with yersh folly,
May long be yersh daysh on thish tresh-shiul ball
And may every shecund be jolly.

113

When Mother Made Angel Cake

WHEN mother baked an angel cake we kids
  would gather round
  An' watch her gentle hands at work, an'
  never make a sound;
We'd watch her stir the eggs an' flour an' powdered
  sugar, too,
An' pour it in the crinkled tin, an' then when it was
  through
She'd spread the icing over it, an' we knew very soon
That one would get the plate to lick, an' one would
  get the spoon.

It seemed no matter where we were, those mornings,
  at our play,
Upstairs or out of doors somewhere, we all knew right
  away
When Ma was in the kitchen, an' was gettin' out the
  tin
An' things to make an angel cake, an' so we scampered
  in.
An' Ma would smile at us an' say: "Now you keep
  still an' wait
An' when I'm through I'll let you lick the spoon an'
  icing plate."

We watched her kneel beside the stove, an' put her
  arm so white
Inside the oven just to find if it was heatin' right.
An' mouths an' eyes were open then, becoz we always
  knew
The time for us to get our taste was quickly comin' due.
Then while she mixed the icing up, she'd hum a simple
  tune,
An' one of us would bar the plate, an' one would bar
  the spoon.

Could we catch a glimpse of Heaven, and some snow-
  white kitchen there,
I'm sure that we'd see mother, smiling now, and still
  as fair;

And I know that gathered round her we should see an
    angel brood
That is watching every movement as she makes an
    angel food;
For I know that little angels, as we used to do, await
The moment when she lets them lick the icing spoon
    and plate.

War

THE thrill of war's a base deceit,
    The rattle of the drum's a lie;
    It lures brave men with scurrying feet
To go where many dangers fly;
It sings a soldier's death is sweet,
    It tells how great it is to die.

And yet no death can splendid be
    That's caused by selfishness and pride;
The weeping widow! Does not she
    Long for the husband at her side?
Can any selfish victory
    Restore the loved one. that has died?

To die for others may be fine,
    But not to die for others' gain;
The thin and faltering battle line,
    The dead men on the bloody plain
Are seldom there by God's design;
    Some human soul must wear the stain.

Murder in uniform, is war,
    Exalted only by a thrill;
And how long must it be before
    Men will not blindly rush to kill?
How many generations more
    Before the cannon's voice is still?

A Boy at Christmas

IF I could have my wish tonight, it would not
    be for wealth or fame,
    It would not be for some delight that men
who live in luxury claim;
But it would be that I might rise at three or four
    a. m. to see,
With eager, happy, boyish eyes, my presents on the
    Christmas tree.
Throughout this world there is no joy, I know now
    I am growing gray,
So rich as being just a boy, a little boy on Christmas
    Day.

I'd like once more to stand and gaze enraptured on a
    tinseled tree,
With eyes that know just how to blaze, a heart still
    tuned to ecstasy;
I'd like to feel the old delight, the surging thrills within
    me come;
To love a thing with all my might, to grasp the
    pleasure of a drum;
To know the meaning of a toy—a meaning lost to
    minds blase;
To be just once again a boy, a little boy on Christmas
    Day.

I'd like to see a pair of skates the way they looked to
    me back then,
Before I'd turned from boyhood's gates and marched
    into the world of men;
I'd like to see a jackknife, too, with those same eager,
    dancing eyes
That couldn't fault or blemish view; I'd like to feel
    the same surprise,
The pleasure, free from all alloy, that has forever
    passed away,
When I was just a little boy and had my faith in
    Christmas Day.

Oh, little, laughing, roguish lad! the king that rules
across the sea
Would give his scepter if he had such joy as now
belongs to thee!
And beards of gray would give their gold and all the
honors they possess
Once more within their grasp to hold thy present fee
of happiness.
Earth sends no greater, surer joy, as, too soon, thou,
as I, shall say,
Than that of his who is a boy, a little boy on Christ-
mas Day.

The Change

SHE'S married to him now, and so
    She doesn't think it worth her while
    To put herself out much to show
Her charming ways or pleasant smile.

She doesn't dress to please him now,
    Nor try to gratify each whim;
She's married to him anyhow,
    There is no need to fuss for him.

Time was she always looked her best
    And did her best to please him, too;
Her voice was of the cheeriest,
    Her whimperings were very few.

She doesn't dress for him today,
    His likes she pays but little heed to,
It makes no difference, anyway,
    She's married, and she doesn't need to.

The Road Builder

I DO not care for garments fine,
　　I do not care for medals bright;
　　I have no wish to quench with wine
　My thirst when I go home at night.
I'm satisfied with work to do,
　　And I'm content to bear my load
If only I can carve and hew
　　For those I love a better road.

I have no wish for luxury
　　If I must live it all alone;
Nor do I toil that I may be
　　By many strangers better known.
If I were here to toil for self
　　I'd have a very simple code,
And I'd need very little pelf—
　　But I'm the builder of a road.

I'm on this earth to pioneer
　　For those who follow after me,
According to my service here
　　Their chance for splendid life will be.
Into the future I must tread
　　Nor whimper at the present goad;
'Tis mine to blaze the path ahead,
　　I am the builder of a road.

I dare not shirk what task I find,
　　I dare not falsely step aside,
Nor leave the tangled brush behind.
　　My pathway must be clear and wide.
For they will tread the way I go,
　　They'll come to reap the seed I sowed
When I am sleeping 'neath the snow,
　　I am the builder of a road.

It is for them I face the front
　　And strive to keep my pathway straight,

It is for them I bear the brunt
    Of selfishness and bitter hate.
That they may know a smoother way,
    That they may bear a lighter load,
I, smiling, face the heat of day—
    I am the builder of a road.

The March o' Man

DOWN to work o' mornings, an' back to home
        at nights,
    Down to hours o' labor, an' home to sweet
        delights;
Down to care an' trouble, an' home to love an' rest,
With every day a good one, an' every evening blest.

Down to dreary dollars, an' back to home to play,
From love to work an' back to love, so slips the day
        away;
From babies back to business an' back to babes again,
From parting kiss to welcome kiss, this marks the
        march o' men.

Some care between our laughter, a few hours filled
        with strife,
A time to stand on duty, then home to babes and wife;
The bugle sounds o' mornings to call us to the fray,
But sweet an' low 'tis love that calls us home at close
        of day.

The Lanes of Apple Bloom

DOWN the lanes of apple bloom, we are treading
    once again,
    Down the pathways rosy red trip the
    women-folk and men.
Love and laughter lead us on, light of heart as children
    gay,
June is smiling on us now, bidding us to romp and play.

Sun-kissed now are maiden's curls, bare of head the
    children run,
Love and laughter call us home when the long day's
    toil is done;
All our cares are borne away on the breezes, perfume
    sweet,
Down the lanes of apple bloom now we dance with
    flying feet.

Through the open door once more comes the pleasant
    breath of June,
Through the open windows now lullabies that mothers
    croon,
Caught upon the evening breeze, reach the toilers
    homeward bound;
Love and laughter rule the world, happiness once more
    is found.

Down the lanes of apple bloom gray-tressed age goes
    walking now
Minding less the weight of years or the wrinkles in
    its brow.
'Tis the evening hour of life, gloriously calm and sweet
June is dwelling in the heart! June is guiding weary
    feet.

The Little Chap

DO you know why men dig ditches
    And why others till the soil?
    Do you know why men seek riches,
    And each morn go out to toil?
It's because at home there's waiting
    Till the busy day is through
Some such sunny, captivating
    Little fellow just like you.

Do you know why one seeks money
    And another tries for fame?
It's to pay for bread and honey
    For the tot that bears his name.
Back of everything men tackle,
    Back of everything men do
You will find the merry cackle
    Of a little chap like you.

Men have, smiling, gone to battle,
    Men have mastered all their fears
Just because their baby's prattle
    Still was ringing in their ears.
And when all the fates were smiting
    They kept on with purpose true,
Undiscouraged.   They were fighting
    For a little chap like you.

So that's why I care for money,
    Why I work the long day through;
It's to pay for bread and honey
    For a little chap like you.
Back of each goal I'm pursuing,
    Back of everything I do,
Is the gurgling and the gooing
    Of a little chap like you.

My Proud Pa

I 'SPOSE the big head bendin' over my crib
            Is my Pa.
     I 'spose that wiseacre whose talk is so glib
            Is my Pa.
I've not been here long—my days are but three,
But there's something that even a baby can see,
An' the man who takes all of the credit for me
            Is my Pa.

I 'spose that the man with the hat that won't fit
            Is my Pa.
I 'spose that the fellow who thinks he is it
            Is my Pa.
He's a little guy, too, but as proud as can be,
An' the wonderful lady an' I both agree
That the one who takes all of the credit for me
            Is my Pa.

I 'spose that the man with that face-stretching grin
            Is my Pa.
I 'spose that the short chap, so terribly thin
            Is my Pa.
My Ma is that wonderful lady in white,
Her voice is as sweet as an angel at night,
Now I'm next to that proud little geezer, all right!
            He's my Pa.

The Women of the Sailors

THE women of the sailors, unto them, O God, be
    kind!
    They never hear the breaking waves, they
    never hear the wind
But that their hearts are anguish-tossed, and every
    thought's a fear,
For the women of the sailors it's a bitter time of year.

The women of the sailors, unto them, O God, be good!
'Tis they who know and understand how frail are steel
    and wood;
'Tis they who never see the spray upon a rock-bound
    coast
But what they breathe a prayer to Thee for those
    that love them most.

The women of the sailors, unto them, O God, be
    nigh!
They never hear the hurricane but that it means a
    sigh;
They never hear the tempest but that they pray to
    Thee
For the safety of their loved ones who are battling with
    the sea.

Neglected

I DON'T get much attention now,
   Although I'm not complaining;
   I'm forced to get on anyhow,
Another king is reigning.
She doesn't run to wait on me,
   However rushed I may be,
Whene'er I need assistance, she
   Is busy with the baby.

Time was my shirts were all laid out
   And all my duds were handy;
And those were days, without a doubt,
   When things were fine and dandy;
But now the time she gave to me
   She's giving to another,
It keeps her busy just to be
   A fond and doting mother.

Oh, I cut quite a figure then,
   To something I amounted;
I stood above all other men,
   With her, I, only, counted.
Then, often I was petted, too,
   And cheered when things went badly;
But now another's come to woo
   And I'm neglected sadly.

And now I come and go each day,
   Just merely tolerated;
And often I am in the way,
   As she has plainly stated.
My wants I'm forced to fill myself,
   However hard it may be;
Oh, I've been put upon the shelf,
   And put there by a baby.

And yet upon that shelf I'd stay,
    And all complainings smother;
The lad who took my wife away
    Has given me his mother.
And every night I kneel and pray
    That never will the day be
That I shall fail to hear her say:
    "I'm busy with the baby!"

The Departed

IF no one ever went ahead,
    If we had seen no friend depart
    And mourned him for a while as dead,
How great would be our fear to start.

If no one for us led the way,
    No loved one, garbed in angel white
Stood there, a welcome word to say,
    Then we should fear the Heavenly flight.

If we should never say "good bye,"
    Should never shed the parting tear,
We'd face the journey to the sky
    In horrible despair and fear.

It is because our friends have gone
    And left us in this vale of breath,
Because of those who've journeyed on,
    That we can bravely smile at death.

A Greeting

OLD friend o'mine, it's Christmas Day
    An' I am thinkin' of you
    An' hopin' that no patch of gray
  Will hide the blue above you.
An' if I had the power to do
    The many things I yearn to,
With joy I'd be surrounding you,
And always when your work is through
    There'd be a kiss to turn to.

You'd never know a single care
    To cause a minute's worry,
There'd be no road you couldn't fare,
    An' do it in a hurry.
I'd clip the thorns from every rose
    You get your fingers on to;
An' warm would be each breeze that blows,
An' each night rare with sweet repose,
    Could I do what I want to.

An' when you sigh for coins of gold,
    I'd fill your purse with money,
An' make each pathway where you strolled
    A bright one an' a sunny.
To friend, I'd change each foe to you,
    The hand upraised to strike, to
One stretched out in friendship true
I'd turn, if this old heart could do
    The things 'twould really like to.

Service

WE know not how we came to be
        Cast for the work that we are doing,
    Why one should sail the stormy sea,
    And one the farmer's horse be shoeing.
Why one should paint and one should write,
    Why one seem dull, another smart;
We only know, both day and night,
    That each of us must play his part.

He serves this world who digs the ditch
    As much as he who writes the novels;
Life leans no more upon the rich
    Than on the men who dwell in hovels.
What greatness is we cannot say,
    God only knows who meets the test;
On earth it's but a part we play,
    And with it each must do his best.

Not a Money Debt

YOU can't pay back in dollars what your father
        does for you,
    You can't repay in kindness all the tender-
        ness he shows;
You little know the perils he has safely brought you
        through,
    And the wealth of Rockefeller this account would
        never close.

Just remember, as you travel, now alone upon your
        way
    That your only chance of squaring up the debt
        you owe your dad
Is to strive with all your courage to grow better every
        day
    And become the man he dreamed of when you
        were a little lad.

127

Out at Pelletier's

OUT at Pelletier's where the blooded pigeons
fly,
 An' the tony Shetland ponies romp and play,
Where the peacock on the fence rail hoots at motors
 chugging by
 An' the wolf hounds at the moon (in Russian)
 bay;
Where the poultry sort o' swaggers in its best blue-
 ribbon style,
 An' the hogs wear silver buttons in their ears,
It is comfortin' an' soothin' jes' to sit an' rest awhile,
 For it brushes back at least a dozen years.

Out at Pelletier's—where old Monte Mark is king,
 An' he knows it an' he shows it to 'em all,
Whether rompin' in the pasture, or in trappings for
 the ring,
 Or whinnyin' to greet you in his stall;
An' where Chief, the son of Monte, in a splendid coat
 of bay
 Shows the heritage of vigor in his veins; ·
It is soothin' an' consolin' to be restin' for a day,
 An' forget the city's dismal grind for gains.

It's a lesson in good breedin'—at the farm o'
 Pelletier's,
 It's a lesson in refinement an' in care;
An' it sets a thinkin' feller sort o' thinkin' o' the
 years
 That are waitin' in the future over there.
An' while he's sittin' restin' underneath the wal-
 nut tree,
 He is thinkin' thoughts perhaps he never speaks;
What's he goin' to leave behind him when his spirit is
 set free?
 Is it money or perfection that he seeks?

Is he strivin' here for dollars or a better human race,
 Just as Pelletier is doin' with his stock?

Would he rather leave a brighter, clearer, smilin'
    boyish face
Than his name upon a massive building rock?
Is he buildin' here for soundness an' for cleanliness of
    heart?
Is he breedin' here for happiness or tears?
Oh, it's good for any feller just to take himself apart
    An' think the thoughts that come at Pelletier's.

He Struck Me!

HE struck me!
    A man I scarce knew, 'though he had
        my name,
Came into my office repeating the same,
And talked for a moment of this and of that;
Remarked that he thought I was putting on fat;
Referred to the weather, repeated a tale
That I laughed at because 'twas exceedingly stale,
And then when I said: "I am busy today,
Whatever you've come for I wish you would say;"
        He struck me.

        He struck me!
He struck me without any reason at all,
For a second I staggered and thought I should fall;
This stranger who'd asked of the health of my wife,
My cousins and aunts, and had picked up my knife
To manicure nicely his finger nails, while
He used up my time in his own breezy style;
But I said: "Make it short. I am busy;" and then
        He struck me—
Yes, boldly he struck me—for ten!

A Creed

LET me be a little kinder,
　　Let me be a little blinder
　　　　To the faults of those around me,
Let me praise a little more;
Let me be, when I am weary
Just a little bit more cheery,
Let me serve a little better
Those that I am striving for.

Let me be a little braver
When temptation bids me waver,
Let me strive a little harder
To be all that I should be;
Let me be a little meeker
With the brother that is weaker,
Let me think more of my neighbor
And a little less of me.

Let me be a little sweeter,
Make my life a bit completer
By doing what I should do
Every minute of the day;
Let me toil, without complaining,
Not a humble task disdaining,
Let me face the summons calmly
When death beckons me away.

A Friend's Greeting

DIAMONDS wouldn't tell yer all I really think
    of you,
        The costliest gift the goldsmith makes I'm
        sure would never do.
There's nothing known that gold can buy that I could
    ever send
That could explain how glad I am to have yer fer a
    friend.

If I had all the wealth of earth and what I like could
    get
And I should send it on to you, I'd still be in your debt,
And still the heart o' me would cry: "That ain't
    enough t' do
Fer one whose smiles an' kindly words have meant so
    much t' you."

It's Christmas time, an' here I am, a-wishin' all that's
    good
Fer you an' yours. A patch o' blue above your
    neighborhood,
The bloom o' health forever on the cheeks o' those you
    love,
An' future years t' bring the joys that now you're
    dreamin' of.

"God bless yer!" That expresses it in simple words
    an' true,
It's what the heart o' me would say if it could speak
    t' you.
May every day be Christmas Day until your journey's
    end,
Is jus' the simple wish of one who's glad you call him
    friend.

The Lost Purse

I REMEMBER the excitement and the terrible
        alarm
    That worried everybody when William broke
        his arm;
An' how frantic Pa and Ma got only jes' the other day
When they couldn't find the baby coz he'd up an'
        walked away.
But I'm sure there's no excitement that our house
        has ever shook
Like the times Ma can't remember where she's put her
        pocketbook.

When the laundry man is standin' at the door an'
        wants his pay
Ma hurries in to get it, an' the fun starts right away.
She hustles to the sideboard coz she's knows exactly
        where
She can put her hand right on it, but alas! it isn't
        there.
She tries the parlor table an' she goes upstairs to look,
An' once more she can't remember where she put her
        pocketbook.

She tells us that she had it just a half an hour ago,
An' now she cannot find it though she's hunted high
        and low;
She's searched the kitchen cupboard an' the bureau
        drawers upstairs,
An' it's not behind the sofa nor beneath the parlor
        chairs.
She makes us kids get busy searching every little nook,
An' this time says she's certain that she's lost her
        pocketbook.

She calls Pa at the office an' he laughs I guess, for then
She always mumbles something 'bout the heartless-
        ness of men.
She calls to mind a peddler who came to the kitchen
        door
An' she's certain from his whiskers an' the shabby
        clothes he wore

132

An' his dirty shirt an' collar that he must have been
    a crook,
An' she's positive that feller came an' got her
    pocketbook.

But at last she allus finds it in some queer an' funny
    spot,
Where she'd put it in a hurry, an' had somehow clean
    forgot;
An' she heaves a sigh of gladness, an' she says, "Well,
    I declare,
I would take an oath this minute that I never put it
    there."
An' we're peaceable an' quiet till next time Ma goes
    to look
An' finds she can't remember where she put her
    pocketbook.

The Monument of Kindness

WE do not build our monuments in stone,
    The records of our life aren't cast in
        steel;
We are forgot, if when the spirit's flown
    No human hearts our finger prints reveal.

If we have lived and died and left behind
    No more than gold and lands that once were ours,
No trace of having served our fellow kind
    Then wasted were our talents and our powers.

But if when we have gone our impress stays
    On human hearts, whate'er has been our lot,
We need no marble shafts to mark our ways,
    We shall live on, nor ever be forgot.

Old-Fashioned Folks

OLD-FASHIONED folks! God bless
    'em all!
    The fathers an' the mothers,
The aunts an' uncles, fat an' tall,
    The sisters an' the brothers.
The good old-fashioned neighbors, too,
    The passing time improves 'em,
They still drop in to chat with you
    Whene'er the spirit moves 'em.
The simple, unaffected folks
    With gentle ways an' sunny,
      The brave an' true
      That live life through
    An' stay unspoiled by money.

Old-fashioned folks, of solid worth,
    On them a benediction!
The joy an' comfort of the earth,
    Its strength, without restriction.
The charm of every neighborhood,
    The toilers uncomplaining,
The men an' women, pure an' good,
    Of fine an' honest graining.
The plain an' open-hearted folks
    That make no fad a passion,
      The kind an' fair
      That do an' dare
    An' are not slaves to fashion.

Old-fashioned folks, that live an' love
    An' give their service gladly,
An' deem their neighbors worthy of
    Their help when things go badly.
The simple sharers of our joys,
    Sweet ministers in sorrow,
They help the world to keep its poise
    An' strength for each tomorrow.

The simple, unaffected folks,
That live for all about 'em,
God bless 'em all,
This earthly ball
Would dreary be without 'em.

Strange

HE thought that he'd be happy if a fortune he
could make,
If he were rich he thought that he'd be gay,
He often thought it would be nice an ocean trip to take
Whenever he desired to go away.

He thought he'd be contented if he owned a motor car
And had the price to pay for gasoline;
He thought he'd like it to afford a fifty-cent cigar
And spend his time a-golfing on the green.

He used to say that he'd be glad if he could ever wear
The latest styles as soon as they appear,
He had a notion that if he were but a millionaire
His life would be one constant round of cheer.

He fell into a fortune. Now a millionaire is he,
The luxuries he yearned for all are his;
But is he quite as happy as he thought he'd really be?
Well, judging from appearances, he is.

Queer Ebenezer

THE strangest man I ever knew
   Is Ebenezer Pettigrew;
      Dropped in on him last night t' chat
Of politics an' this an' that,
An' when he'd showed me to a seat
He brung some apples in t' eat,
An' tuk one up, an' stroked its side
An' fondled it t' show his pride.
Says I t' him: "It's plain t' me
Thet things ain't what they orter be;
Men ain't as honest as they wuz,
Vice profits more'n virtue does,
The weak are downtrod by the strong,
The whole world's overrun by wrong."
An' then I showed him facts t' prove
Thet we air gettin' in a groove
O' wickedness, an' steeped in sin,
But all he did wuz work his chin
A-chewin' on his apple core
An' lookin' at his parlor floor,
An' then, says he, right slow t' me:
"Some things ain't what they orter be,
But still I ain't inclined to pine,
Apples this year air mighty fine."

He tuk another pippin then
An' started in t' chew again.
"Now Eb," says I, "Ye've got t' say
Thet we air in a dreadful way;
Thet life is full o' pain an' woe,
An' rough air roads thet we must go.
The iron heels of lust and greed
Air on our necks, an' if you read
The papers nowadays, you'll note
Thet rumors dreadful air afloat;
Our judges ain't exactly just
In matters that affect a trust."
I put it to him good an' strong,

Expectin' that he'd come erlong
An' jine with me by nod or sign,
But nary nod or move t' jine
He made, but turnin' in his chair
An' reachin' fer the table, where
An old brown pitcher stood, says he:
"Come on an' have a drink with me;
I ain't denyin' what you say,
It mebbe things air thataway,
But here's yer glass, now ain't that clear?
The cider's mighty fine this year."

A Song

KEEP the heart laughin' in spite o' the tears,
  Keep the heart youthful in spite o' the years,
  Keep your faith shinin' in spite o' the night
That comes down with sorrows, and you'll be all right.

Keep the hand steady, and keep the hand true,
Keep your work blameless whatever you do;
Keep your life clean, as you wander along,
An' no matter what happens you cannot go wrong.

Knee deep in sorrow, an' knee deep in care,
Still keep on hopin' an' whisper your prayer;
Keep your faith shinin' an' tread on your way,
An' peace an' contentment will find you some day.

A Discussion

SHE put her arms about my neck,
 And whispered low to me:
  "I'm thinking daddy, dear, how nice
And lovely it would be
If only every little girl
 In all this wide world through
Had daddies that were just as nice
 And kind and good as you."

And then I took her in my arms
 And held her on my knee
And said: "A nicer, brighter world
 I'm sure that it would be
If only every grown-up man
 Beneath the skies of blue
Were daddy to a little girl
 As nice and sweet as you."

A Prayer

I DO not ask a level road
 Always to tread,
  Nor do I ask a trifling load
Of care and dread.
I do not pray that I may be
 Spared all of rain
Of darkness and anxiety
 And bitter pain.

I do not pray for favors great,
 Nor would I shun
The tasks or sorrows that await
 Tomorrow's sun.
But I do pray for strength to bear
 From day to day
Without complaint, my bit of care
 Along the way.

138

Living Monuments

OUR children are our monuments,
     The little ones we leave behind,
     If they are good and brave and
          kind,
And labor here with true intents,
     Our lives and work perpetuate
     Far more than marble tablets great.

Far rather would I pass away
     And leave a sturdy son of mine,
     Whom I had taught to love the fine,
The just and honest; in his day
     To serve the world with courage bold,
     Than have my life on granite told.

I'd rather feel when death is near
     That in my children I shall live;
     No monument of stone would give
Me greater glory, year by year,
     Than sons and daughters treading on
     In truth and honor when I'm gone.

Who leaves a sturdy son on earth,
     A noble daughter, sweet and pure,
     Has monuments that long endure.
He needs no shaft to prove his worth;
     The luster of his children's deeds
     Are all the monuments he needs.

The Joy of Getting Back

THERE ain't the joy in foreign skies that those
    of home possess,
      An' friendliness o' foreign folks ain't home-
    town friendliness;
An' far-off landscapes with their thrills don't grip me
    quite as hard
As jes' that little patch o' green that's in my own back-
    yard.

It's good to feel a stranger's hand grip heartily your
    own,
It's good to see a stranger's smile when you are all
    alone;
But though a stranger's grip is warm, an' though his
    smile is sweet
There's something in the home folks' way that has the
    stranger's beat.

A railroad train that's outward bound bears many a
    man an' dame
Who think a thousand miles away the sunsets brighter
    flame;
An' seekin' joys they think they lack they pack their
    grips an' roam,
An' just as I, they some day find the sweetest joys at
    home.

Away from home the girls are fair an' men are kind of
    heart,
An' there you'll always find a few who sigh when you
    depart,
But though you rode a million miles o'er gleaming
    railroad track
You'd never find a joy to beat the joy of gettin' back.

Punishment

THEIR childhood is so brief that we
  Should hesitate to spoil their fun,
  We should be very slow to see
  The things that they should not have done.
For such a little while they play
  Before the rough, long roads they tread,
We should be careful every day
  To send no weeping child to bed.

So soon they'll women be and men,
  With all the cares that grown-ups know,
We should be slow to punish, when
  Their little feet in mischief go.
Our whippings should be very few,
  Yes, very few, and very mild,
We should be careful what we do
  In dealing with a happy child.

So few the years that are their own,
  So brief the time to romp and play,
So very quickly are they grown
  To face the battles of the day
That we should hesitate to mar
  With punishment, however slight,
The days that oh, so precious are,
  And turn to grief a child's delight.

Too soon will come the long days when
  They'll often heavy-hearted be,
And they'll look back on childhood then
  And think of you and think of me.
And we should have them then recall
  When we are sleeping in the grave
Not how we punished children small,
  But how we kissed them and forgave.

Jes' Wonderin'!

I WONDER if they're bitin' way off yonder in
    the bay!
    I wonder if they're fightin' very hard t' git
      away!
I wonder if they're hungry, an' would grab a silver
    spoon
Th' way that I remember they used t' do in June!
I wonder if Ole Daddy's caught his big one yet this
    year;
An' I guess the boss is wonderin' why I'm sittin' idle
    here.

I wonder if the lily pads are just as thick t'day
As what they were in by-gone times when I was on
    the bay!
I wonder if my favorite spot right now is occupied
By some one else, an' if it's come t' be a stranger's
    pride;
An' if he knows its secrets, too, an' holds 'em just as
    dear,
An' if the boss is wonderin' why I'm sittin' wonderin'
    here.

I wonder if the gulls fly 'round the way they used t'
    do,
T' grab the minnows now an' then that in the bay I
    threw!
I wonder if I still could cast as true as what I did
When I could land it every time where some big one
    was hid!
An' O, I wonder if the day will ever come again
When I shall hear a singing reel, the way I heard it
    then.

Tell Him Why

WHEN your boy wants to do what he
    shouldn't—
      Some foolish or dangerous thing.
Or something you wish that he wouldn't,
    A deed that disaster may bring,
That he must not you hasten to tell him
    And threaten him should he defy,
With a positive order you quell him,
    But do you explain to him why?

When you want him to do what he should do,
    When you're eager to have him polite,
When its something you know that he could do,
    Do you train him with reason or fright?
You may say that he "must" or severely
    With him you will deal by and by;
You see why it's proper most clearly,
    But do you explain to him why?

A boy's mind is open to reason,
    A thinking device is his brain;
Injustice he's ready to seize on,
    So why don't you stop to explain?
It's perfectly proper to check him
    When you see that in danger he'd fly,
But it certainly sure that you'll wreck him
    Unless you explain to him why.

Ma an' Me

THERE'VE been times we'd disagree
    Somethin' awful, Ma an' me;
    Times when I would bang the door
Never to come back no more,
An' go stompin' down the street
Sayin' things I won't repeat;
Vowin' that the only course
For us two was a di-vorce.
Then when it come time for tea
We'd make up, would Ma an' me.

We've had many a lively spat
Arguin' over this an' that.
There've been times when Ma got mad,
Said enough o' me she'd had,
Tired o' listenin' to me jaw;
Reckoned that she'd go t' law,
Tell the judge her tale o' woe,
An' my own way I could go.
Then the children we would see
An' we'd laugh, would Ma an' me.

Ma an' me ain't angels quite,
Neither of us does things right.
She's got reason fer complaint,
She ain't married to a saint;
Guess I've tried her patience more
Than the children round the door;
An' at times, by all that's fine,
Ma has certainly tried mine.
But together still are we,
Pals an' lovers—Ma an' me.

We've just plodded on the way
Hand in hand from day to day,
Workin' for the greatest good,
Doin' just the best we could.
Gettin' mad, as people will,
But remainin' faithful still.

An' we've never gone to bed
Till we took back all we said,
Kissed, an' vowed we'd always be
Pals an' sweethearts—Ma an' me.

Lines to the Wash Woman

LADY, when you say you'll come
    Tuesday morn to do our washing,
    Tell us if there isn't some
Way to know if you are joshing?

When you promise to be here
    Toiling at our tubs and wringers,
And we think you are sincere,
    Tell us, do you cross your fingers?

When we show you round our place,
    And you vow you'll come and clean it,
How, we ask you to your face,
    Can we know you really mean it?

You with promises are glib,
    This we do not say to grieve you,
But so many times you fib,
    Tell us when can we believe you?

Lady, when we rise at six,
    Just to get the water boiling,
We are in a sorry fix
    When you dodge your day of toiling.

All your failures leave us glum,
    It's a shame to waste a day so,
If you do not mean to come,
    Why on earth do you not say so?

Answering Age

AGE is calling to me, with his finger long and
    grim,
      It is urging me to wander down the dreary
    lanes with him,
It has lined my cheeks with furrows, and has tinged
    my hair with gray,
And is ever whispering to me that I've grown too old
    to play;
But the heart of me keeps saying, "Let us dance our
    way along,
Let us answer age with laughter, let us drive him off
    with song."

Age comes to me saying: "You are mine forever more,
It is vain for you to hunger for the joys you knew of
    yore.
Now the feet of you are weary, and the eyes of you
    are dim,
Come with me, my worn-out brother, come and share
    my dwelling grim."
But the heart of me keeps saying: "I will cling to
    youth for you,
I will keep you in the sunshine where the skies are
    always blue.

"Give to age your cheeks for furrows, let him silver, if
    he will.
The hair about your temples, but I'll keep you
    youthful still;
Let him dull your eyes, if need be, weight your feet
    with bygone years,
But I'll wake you with my singing, when the break
    of day appears,
I will fill your days with laughter, and with roses
    strew your way,
Say to age you do not fear him, while your heart is
    young and gay."

Contentment

I TAKE it as I go along
　　That life must have its gloom,
　　That now and then the sound of song
Must fade from every room;
That every heart must know its woe,
　　Each door death's sable sign,
Care falls to every one, and so
　　I strive to bear with mine.

Misfortune is a part of life;
　　No one who journeys here
Can dodge the bitterness of strife
　　Or pass without a tear.
Love paves the way for us to mourn,
　　Our pleasures breed regret,
One day a sparkling joy is born,
　　The next—our eyes are wet.

Each life is tinctured with the pain
　　Of sorrow and of care,
As now and then come clouds and rain,
　　Come hours of despair.
And yet the sunshine bursts anew,
　　And those who weep shall smile,
For joy is always breaking through
　　In just a little while.

It Couldn't Be Done

SOMEBODY said that it couldn't be done
    But he with a chuckle replied
    That "maybe it couldn't," but he would
        be one
    Who wouldn't say so till he'd tried.
So he buckled right in with the trace of a grin
    On his face. If he worried he hid it.
He started to sing as he tackled the thing
    That couldn't be done, and he did it!

Somebody scoffed: "Oh, you'll never do that
    At least no one ever has done it;"
But he took off his coat and he took off his hat
    And the first thing we knew he'd begun it.
With a lift of his chin and a bit of a grin,
    Without any doubting or quiddit,
He started to sing as he tackled the thing
    That couldn't be done, and he did it.

There are thousands to tell you it cannot be done,
    There are thousands to prophesy failure,
There are thousands to point out to you one by one,
    The dangers that wait to assail you.
But just buckle in with a bit of a grin,
    Just take off your coat and go to it;
Just start in to sing as you tackle the thing
    That "cannot be done," and you'll do it.

Money

I'D hate to think so much of gold
    That I would sell myself to gain it,
I'd hate the sound of metal cold
    If I must shamefully attain it.
I'd hate to be so much a slave
    To minted silver, gold and copper,
That I'd forget in moments grave
    To do the decent thing and proper.

I'd like to live a life of ease,
    And tread a pathway always sunny,
But I'd not worship on my knees
    The golden idol known as Money.
A man of wealth I'd like to be,
    But I would rather dig in ditches
Than ever have it said of me,
    I'd sold my self-respect for riches.

A Greeting

IF every day of yours were fine
    And every sky of yours were blue,
You couldn't know such joy of mine,
    The joy o' being friend to you.

You've brushed away the clouds of care
    And often dried the bitter tears,
And left a debt I couldn't square
    If I should live a thousand years.

I'm wishing you'll as happy be
    As I am all this journey through,
Who have this joy to comfort me,
    The joy o' being friend to you.

A Personal View of War

I NEVER pondered much on war,
    Except to think it was inspiring
To have a cause to battle for,
    To hear the guns and cannons firing;
To see brave men rush up to death
    Without a sign or trace of terror,
To give their country blood and breath,
    But now I know it's all an error;
War is a frightful thing I know,
What if my boy should have to go?

Last night I leaned above his crib
    And spent a little while in playing,
I tickled him beneath his bib,
    And watched his little body swaying
With innocent delight, and then
    It seemed I heard the noise of battle,
The wails and shrieks of dying men,
    The cannons' boom, the muskets' rattle,
And shuddered as I stooped down low,
What if my babe some day must go?

War did not seem a splendid thing,
    There was no glory in the fighting,
No thrill in hearing bullets sing,
    No joy in men each other smiting.
I saw but heartache, and the grave,
    And misery and desolation,
As splendid fellows, bold and brave,
    Were sacrificed unto the nation;
I wept with men of long ago
Whose boys marched out to face the foe.

I used to think that war was grand
    That bugle calls were splendid, thrilling;
But now I know and understand,
    They sound the message to start killing.
And when I ponder now on war
    'Tis but to see the terror of it,

The glory that I saw before
  Has vanished in the error of it.
War may have seemed a brilliant show,
It's different when your own may go!

Troubles

TROUBLES? Sure I've lots of them,
    Got 'em heaped up by the score,
    Got 'em baled and bundled up,
  Got 'em hid behind the door.
Got 'em young and got 'em old,
    Got 'em big and little, too.
Don't care to discuss 'em now,
    Rather tell my joys to you.

Got the finest home there is,
    Got the finest pair o' boys,
An' the sweetest little girl,
    Reg'lar livin', breathin' joys.
Got the finest wife in town,
    Got a little garden, too.
Troubles? Sure I've got 'em, but
    Rather tell my joys to you.

Got a bunch of friends I love,
    Friends I know are staunch and true;
Visit 'em, they visit me,
    Jus' the way good friends should do;
Got my health, an' got a job,
    That's enough to see me through.
Troubles? Sure I've got 'em, but
    Rather tell my joys to you.

At the Wedding

THERE was weepin' by the women that the
    crowd could plainly see,
      An' old William's throat was chokin' an' his
eyes were watery,
An' he couldn't hardly answer when the parson made
    him say
Who it was on that occasion was to give the girl away.

I detest tears at a weddin', an' I didn't like 'em then,
An' I couldn't see the reason for the lips that trembled
    when
Reverend Goodly looked about him ere he tied the
    knot to stay
An' said: "Which of you assembled here now gives
    this girl away?"

I shall not forget old William an' the solemn look he
    wore,
Though he tried his best at smilin' I could tell his
    heart was sore;
I could see the tear drops startin' as he looked at
    little May,
An' I knew the wrench it caused him when he gave
    his girl away.

I could hear the women sobbin', an' I didn't dare to
    look,
I jes' kep' my face straight forward till the parson
    closed his book.
For the heart of me was beatin' not in sadness, but
    in glee;
I had reason to be happy. He was givin' her to me.

The Time for Brotherhood

WHEN a fellow's feeling blue,
    And is troubled, through and through
    With a melancholy feeling
That he cannot seem to shake,
When his plans have gone astray
And his hopes have slipped away
And he's standing at the crossroads
Wondering which one to take,
That's the time to grab his hand
And to make him understand
That he's grieving over trifles
And his worries aren't worth while;
That's the time to slap his back
With a good old friendly whack,
That's the time he needs your friendship
And the time he wants your smile.

When he's deep down in the dumps
And has known life's rocky bumps,
When he's got the kill-joy notion
That his work no longer counts;
That's the time a word of cheer
Sweetly whispered in his ear
Sets the heart of him to beating
'Till his spirit proudly mounts.
That's the time a glad "Hello!"
Means far more than you may know,
That's the time a sign of friendship
Really does a brother good;
That's the time a word of praise
Lifts a fellow up for days,
Sends him on his way, rejoicing,
That's the time for brotherhood.

Answering the Grumblers

WHEN night time comes an' I can go
  Back to the folks who love me so,
  An' see 'em smile an' hear 'em sing,
An' feel their kisses, then, by jing!
I vow this world is mighty fine
An' run upon a great design.

I trudge away at break o' day
An' hear the grumblers round me say,
This world ain't what it ought to be,
With so much care an' misery,
An' so much work for all to do,
An' little comfort when you're through.

But all the time I'm thinkin' of
The faces of the ones I love,
An' every minute I can see
Their bright eyes laughing right at me,
An' I can almost hear 'em say:
"Come home, come home, an' we will play."

An' sometimes when the daily grind
Sends bitter thoughts into my mind,
An' I get thinkin' that of care
I draw far more than is my share,
I hear 'em hum their merry song,
An' then I know such thoughts are wrong.

I never doubt this world is good,
I couldn't doubt it if I would
For all the trouble that I meet
I gather compensation sweet
When night time comes an' I can go
Back to the folks who love me so.

It ain't no use for grumblers here
To tell me that this life's severe,
To say this world's a vale of woe,

For I've got proof that it ain't so,
When wearily I trudge away,
They're whisperin', whisperin': "Soon we'll
    play."

Now and Then

WHY not think a decent thought,
    Now and then?
      Why not ponder, as you ought,
Now and then?
Get your mind out of the mire,
To the higher things aspire,
Claim a loftier desire,
    Now and then.

Think of something else than gold,
    Now and then!
Think of things not bought and sold,
    Now and then;
Turn from sordid deeds and mean,
In your acts your thoughts are seen,
Think of something sweet and clean,
    Now and then.

Think of good instead of bad,
    Now and then;
Of the bright things, not the sad,
    Now and then;
If you think the way you should,
As you could think if you would,
You would do a lot of good,
    Now and then.

Happiness

IF the sunbeams will not start you to rejoicing,
　　If the laughter of your babies you can hear
　　Without little songs of gladness gayly voicing,
　If their dancing doesn't drive away your tear;
If you don't find happiness where they are playing,
　　If they do not make your pathways bright and
　　　　sunny,
Then gladness from your heart has gone a-straying
　And you won't be any happier with money.

If the blue skies bending over you don't thrill you,
　If the roses just a-bursting into bloom
With a sense of perfect pleasure do not fill you,
　If the song birds do not chase away your gloom;
If you cannot find contentment in your cottage
　Then your heart for joy has not become a chalice,
If you cannot, smiling, eat your simple pottage,
　Then you'd not be any happier in a palace.

If a troop of healthy, laughing boys and lassies
　Doesn't strike you as a reason to rejoice;
If the glories of the earth, when winter passes,
　You behold and still retain a whining voice;
If it doesn't rouse your spirits to go fishing,
　Then your heart is but a cupboard for despair,
And for money all in vain today you're wishing,
　You'd make a most unhappy millionaire.

Real Help.

IF you can smooth his path a bit,
    Bring laughter to his worried face,
    Restore today his stock of grit
And help him all his troubles chase.
If you can speak one word of praise
That shall his drooping spirits raise
    And warm his heart with cheer,
You have done more than they will do
Who'll sighing, rush some day to strew
    Red roses on his bier.

If you stretch out a hand to him
    Today when he is plodding on,
When everything seems dark and grim,
    And hope is very nearly gone,
If you go to him where he stays
And speak the little word of praise
    That now may banish fear,
You will have done more good than they
Who'll rush to praise his lifeless clay
    And strew with flowers his bier.

If you will note the good you see
    In him today, while yet he lives,
If you will be the friend you'll be
    When death to him the summons gives,
While he is here to hear your praise,
To profit by your kindly ways,
    You'll not seem insincere
If, when death's smile is on his face,
You rush to be the first to place
    Red roses on his bier.

Home

EIGHT rooms and bath, a cellar, too, a little
        patch of mother earth,
    Above it just a stretch of blue, it makes no
        difference what it's worth,
It's home to me, and more and more I grow to love
    it every day,
And when at night I pass the door, it's there I always
    want to stay.

The furniture, perhaps, is not so fine as other folks
    possess,
But it's a mighty cosy spot, and shelters in our
    happiness;
The pictures on the walls aren't much, our tapestries
    aren't extra fine,
But everything I see or touch holds joy for me because
    it's mine.

Within these unpretentious walls are love and laughter
    finely blent;
Rich men may have their marble halls, they cannot
    shut out discontent,
And were this house a mansion grand I could not any
    happier be,
For here I have at my command all that the world
    can give to me.

A Creed

TO live in hearts, not monuments of stone,
  To live on humble lips that nightly pray;
  To be remembered when the soul has flown
As one who smiled and passed along the way.

To leave behind not buildings towering high,
  Nor stacks of gold I made, but couldn't spend,
To be remembered when I've journeyed by
  As one who did his best to be a friend.

To come to death without one wish to keep
  The precious earthly prizes I have won,
But smiling, sink into eternal sleep
  Without regret—at peace with everyone.

History Teaches

CAESAR did a few things,
    Horace wrote in style,
    Good old Plato knew things
  Very much worth while.
Famous Aristotle
    Had the master's touch;
Blow this in your bottle:
    "I am not so much."

Con your history's pages,
    Read the tales of Rome,
Then compare the sages'
    To your feeble dome.
All the dead ones study
    (If you call them such;)
They will teach you, Buddy,
    You are not so much.

Capital Punishment

PROUD is the state of its millions of men,
    And proud is the state of its name;
      In its borders are masters of brush and of pen,
    And wide as the world is its fame.
It stands for the best of the blood of the years,
    Yet an eye for an eye is its way,
And there at the base of its progress appears
    The chamber of murder today.

It has fashioned the visions of ages long gone,
    What were dreams of the past now are real;
Its deserts and hills men have builded upon
    Great structures of stone and of steel.
It is proud of its colleges, splendid and true,
    Where its youth obtain learning and skill;
It has turned from the old to the glorious new,
    But the death house is part of it still.

It boasts of its work in humanity's cause,
    Of its churches with steeples and domes;
And proudly it tells of its numberless laws
    That safeguard its millions of homes.
It has stretched out its hand to the child of the mill,
    It has led him from labor to play;
Yet the chamber of death is a part of it still,
    And some one must murder for pay.

Choking rabbi and priest mutter fear-stifled prayers
    To the great God of mercy above
As the ominous footfalls are heard on the stairs,
    And ask Him for mercy and love.
Oh, mockery! Asking the Master to show
    Compassion, when ye of the state
Stand up and insist on a blow for a blow,
    And murder in legalized hate!

Oh, mockery! Asking the good God to spare
 This man on the brink of the grave,
That ye, as a state, by your actions declare
 Ye haven't found worthy to save.
Ye have shaken the fetters of ages long gone,
 Ye have risen in glory and gain;
How long must the God of us all look upon
 The chamber of death ye maintain?

He Has Not Lived in Vain

HE has not lived in vain
  If men can say
   When he has passed away:
"He labored not for gain."

If one can truly say:
  "I loved him for his smile,
  He walked with me a mile,
And cheered my weary way."

If only one shall stand
  And sadly murmur this:
  "My friend, my friend, I'll miss
The pressure of your hand."

If only this remain:
  One heart that he has cheered;
  His monument is reared,
He has not lived in vain.

A Pat on the Back

A PAT on the back is a wonderful thing,
It gives a man courage to whistle and sing;
When hope is departing, the outlook is grim,
A pat on the back then says volumes to him.
It whispers: "Keep at it! You're doing all right,
Just dig in your toes and get busy and fight,
There's one man behind you, go to it, old man,
One pal who is sure that you can, that you can."

A pat on the back from a stranger or friend
When your jaw starts to sag and your knees start to
bend
Will bring you right up with new courage and grit
And you'll keep in the fight when you were going to
quit,
You'll feel it, you'll hear it—yes, actually hear it—
For hours saying "dig in, old fellow. Don't fear it,
That isn't as hard as it looks. Be a man,
There's a fellow back there who believes that you
can."

Just a pat on the back. And for days and for days,
No matter how far you may roam, it still stays
By your side, and no matter how hard be your fight
It's whispering always: "You'll come out all right.
There's a fellow back there who's believing in you,
Expecting each minute to see you come through
With your colors still flying and leading your clan!"
And the first thing you know you are saying: "I can."

Oh, a pat on the back is a wonderful thing,
The touch of it's magic; I've known it to bring
Back hopes that were fleeting, and strength that
seemed gone
And smiles that had vanished and urge a man on
When it seemed that he couldn't one step advance
more
Till he conquered. And that's what I'm singing this
for;
If you see a poor brother whose nerve's out of whack,
Just step up and give him a pat on the back.

King

(Being an attempt to write it as Tom Daly might do)

GIUSEPPE TOMASSI ees stylisha chap,
    He wear da white collar an' cuff,
    He says: "For expanse I no giva da rap,
Da basta ees not good enough."
When out weeth hees Rosa he wear da silk hat,
    An' carry da cane lik' da lord;
He spenda hees money lik' dees, an' lik' dat,
    For Giuseppe, he work at da Ford.

He smoke da seegar wit da beega da band,
    Da tree-for-da-quart' ees da kind,
Da diamond dat flash from da back of hees hand
    Ees da beegest Giuseppe could find.
He dress up hees Rosa in satin an' lace,
    She no longer scrub at da board,
But putta da paint on da leeps an' da face,
    For Giuseppe, he work at da Ford.

Giuseppe, ees strutta about lik' da keeng,
    An' laugh at da hard-worka man
Who grinda da org' a few neekles to bring
    Or sella da ripa banan'.
Each morning he waxa da blacka moustache
    Then walk up an' down through da ward;
You batta he gotta da playnta da cash,
    For Giuseppe, he work at da Ford.

Lonely

YOU'RE not feeling well today,
     Little Fellow,
       You're not very keen for play,
     Little Fellow;
All you want to do is nap
On your mother's comfy lap
And you lack your vim and snap,
     Little Fellow.

When you're well it's me you pick,
     Little Fellow,
For the romp and roguish trick,
     Little Fellow;
But when you are feeling weak
And the color leaves your cheek,
It's your mother that you seek,
     Little Fellow.

Then you want your mother's breast,
     Little Fellow,
That's the finest place to rest,
     Little Fellow;
When the fever's burning you,
You know, just as once I knew,
Only mother's arms will do,
     Little Fellow.

Now I'm sitting in my den,
     Little Fellow,
Waiting till you come again,
     Little Fellow;
And I hear the gentle croon
Of a sweet and soothing tune,
And I hope you'll get here soon,
     Little Fellow.

Dreading

SOMETIMES when they are tucked in bed the
gentle mother comes to me
And talks about each curly head, and
wonders what they're going to be.
She tells about the fun they've had while I was toiling
far away,
Recalls the bright things that the lad and little girl
have had to say.
Each morning is a pleasure new, and gladness over-
flows the cup,
And then she says: "What will we do, what will we
do when they're grown up?"

She looks about the room and sees the train of cars
beneath the chair,
The soldiers resting at their ease, the wooly dog, the
Teddy bear,
The china doll, the painted ball, the building blocks
about the floor,
And then she smiles to see them all, and even wishes
there were more;
The whole day passes in review, she stoops and strokes
the wooly pup,
And says to me: "What will we do, what will we do
when they're grown up?"

I share with her that self-same dread, a house devoid
of children's toys,
No little tots to put to bed, no romping little girls
and boys;
No little lips to kiss at night, no broken skates or
sleds to mend,
I fear to think that such delight the years will very
quickly end.
Old Age, I dare not look at you, when we alone shall
sit and sup,
I wonder, too, what will we do, what will we do when
they're grown up?

A Real Thriller

WE were speakin' of excitement, an' the hair
    upliftin' thrills
    That sorter dot life's landscape, like the
bill board ads. for pills,
An' one feller spoke of bein' in a railroad wreck or
    two
An' another one of skatin' on some ice that let him
    through.
Then a meek-faced little brother in the smoker's
    corner said:
"I'll admit you folks have suffered temporary fear
    'an dread,
But, tell me, have you ever ridden sixteen miles at
    night
In a livery stable cutter, when the snow was deep an'
    white
An' discovered, when attracted by the lash's singin'
    cuts
That the driver's full of whisky an' the road is full of
    ruts?

"Don't talk to me of terror, 'less you've ridden in a
    sleigh
Through a strange an' barren country, jus' before
    the break o' day
When it's blacker than your derby, an' you're shiver-
    in' with cold
An' the fear that in a minute down a chasm you'll be
    rolled.
I would volplane in a biplane, though I'm not a
    Wilbur Wright,
I would join the crazy Frenchman in his somersault-
    ing flight.
I would even scoff at Villa or some other Greaser
    thug,
An' not worry that my body soon would stop a leaden
    slug.
But I'd pass up midnight riding, where a deep
    ravine abuts

When the driver's full of whisky an' the road is
full of ruts.

"I never for one minute doubt that there's a
Providence,
A wiser power above us, something more than mortal
sense;
A wisdom that is deeper than the wisdom man has
shown,
A mercy that is sweeter than we selfish mortals own.
That there is a God in Heaven is as sure as sure
can be,
An' each day that I am living certain proof of it I see.
If we'd have it manifested, there's no need to go to
schools,
Or to scholars or the sages—we may learn it from the
fools.
One must really be watched over by an eye that
never shuts
When the driver's full of whisky and the road is full
of ruts."

George Moir Black

A FRIEND has passed
Across the bay,
So wide and vast,
And put away
The mortal form
That held his breath;
But through the storm
That men call death,
Erect and straight,
Unstained by years,
At Heaven's gate
A man appears.

Glad

THERE'S a battered old drum on the floor,
     And a Teddy bear sleeps in my chair,
     There's a doll carriage barring the door;
Ah, it's weeks since she trundled it there!
There are building blocks strewn in the hall,
     And a train of cars wrecked on the track,
And I smile as I gaze at them all,
     Thank goodness, the children are back.

There's a handkerchief tied to my cane,
     That's a flag that a soldier boy bears;
Now the yard is a grim battle plain
     And the soldiers are marching in pairs.
There are finger marks now on the wall
     That were left there by hands that were black,
But I smile as I gaze at them all,
     Thank goodness, the children are back.

There are cries of delight and despair
     Resounding once more through the place;
There are pillow fights fierce on the stair,
     And down through the hall there's a race;
There's a bump of a terrible fall
     As the enemy's camp they attack,
But I smile as I list to it all,
     Thank goodness, the children are back.

For give me the clamor and noise
     And give me the pranks that they play,
The disturbance of girls and of boys
     That comes at the end of the day.
For I'm sick of monotony's pall
     That hovered for weeks o'er the shack,
It is music to me when they call,
     Thank goodness, the children are back.

Different

I DON'T believe in worry, and it's foolish to
despair,
And dreading what may happen never lightens
any care;
I believe in facing trouble, without fretting o'er the
cost,
But it's altogether different when your little one is lost.

Oh, it's altogether different when you think she's gone
astray,
When she's toddled from the doorway, and you cannot
tell which way;
When you call and get no answer, and you call and call
again
You are game, but still you worry—for it's mighty
different then.

Then the sweat comes on your forehead, and your
nerves begin to dance,
And the only thing you think of is some dreadful
circumstance.
You never stop to reason, and you play no hero's part,
For terror—trembling terror—is a lodger in your heart.

You could face financial ruin without parting with
your grin,
You could smile to see another take the prize you
hoped to win,
But you never cease to worry till you find your child
again
In the cupboard where she's hiding—for it's mighty
different then.

Contrary Sary

"THERE'S no sense arguin' with 'em," says
      Ebenezer Oates,
    "You can't convince the women that they
      ain't fit fer votes;
There's Sary got the notion that she's as good as man,
An' I can't show her diff'runt, an' no man livin' can.
She's most onreasonubbel. 'Now, I suppose,' says
      she,
'If I got drunk each evenin' ye'd think lots more o'
      me?'

"She's so consarn contrary, she won't talk common
      sense,
She flies right off the handle the minute I commence.
'Of course, we ain't men's equals,' says Sary, 'if we
      wuz
We'd hang around some barroom the way Jim Pilzer
      does;
We'd soak ourselves with liquor, an' guzzle down our
      pay
An' show ourselves your equals in some sich manly
      way.'

"Now what's the use of reason, when women talk like
      that?
Ye might as well keep silent. With facts I knock her
      flat,
But when I git her cornered, she smiles an' says t' me:
'Hank Foss has been arrested. He beat his family;
The neighbors have his children, his wife is sick in
      bed,
The ballot ain't fer wimmin, it's kep' fer Hank in-
      stead.'

"It really is a caution how foolish she's become!
'I wisht I knew enough,' says she, 't' be a village bum;
I wisht I had the brain power t' loaf around all day
An' see my children barefoot, but I ain't built that
      way.

If I wuz some men's equal, then maybe I'd be wise
Enough t' starve my children an' black my dear ones'
    eyes.' "

I'll Never Be Rich

I'LL never be rich.
        I'm too fond of the joy
        Of a certain small girl
And a certain small boy;
And the nights full of fun
And the days full of play,
And the romp and the run
At the end of the day.

        I'll never be rich.
I'm too eager to share
In the joys that are near,
Too unwilling to care
For the thing we call gold,
That I'll fill every day
Full of strife for the stuff,
And not rest by the way.

        I'll never be rich.
There are too many charms
That I now can possess
When I stretch out my arms;
There are too many joys
That already I hold
That I cannot give up
Just to wallow in gold.

For the Living

IF you like a brother here,
Tell him so;
If you hold his friendship dear,
Let him know;
All the roses that you spread
On his bier when he is dead
Are not worth one kind word said
Years ago.

You can help a brother now
If you will
Smooth the furrows from his brow;
You can kill
The despair that's in his heart
With a word, and ease the smart.
So why stand you now apart
Keeping still?

You can help a brother when
He is here;
He would hold your praises then
Very dear.
But absurdly still you stay
And withhold what you could say
That would cheer him on his way
For his bier.

What, I wonder, if the dead
Saw and heard
What is done and what is said
Afterward,
Would they utter in reply?
Would they smile and ask us why,
When the time to help was nigh,
No one stirred?

"Keep your roses for the living,"
    They would say,
"Waste no time in praises giving
    Us today;
Strew some living brother's way so,
If you like another, say so,
For the thing that now you praise so
    Is but clay."

The Lonely Fight

IT'S easy to be right when the multitude is cheering,
    It is easy to have courage when you're fighting
      with the throng;
But it's altogether different when the multitude is
    sneering
    To fight for what you know is right with no one
    else along.

It's easy to be honest when the multitude is gazing,
    It is easy to be truthful when the crowds are
      standing by;
But it's altogether different when there is no spotlight
    blazing
    To stand alone for what is right and never cheat
    or lie.

Answering the Usual Questions

MY name is Johnny Vincent Brown,
    I live on Leicester Court,
      My Pa's not here, he's gone downtown,
An' I am three feet short,
An' I weigh sixty-three pounds, too,
    An' I know my A, B, C's,
An' I say good-bye an' howdy-do,
    An' yessum, yessir, please.

An' I'm a good boy all the time,
    I do jes' what I'm told,
I like ter run an' jump an' climb,
    I'm only four years old.
I don't like hair that hangs in curls,
    An' I am fond of cake,
But I ain't got no use for girls
    An' I hate stummick ache.

I like the baby that we've got,
    I go ter Sunday School,
I say my prayers beside my cot,
    I know the Golden Rule.
I'll be a man when I grow up,
    I've got a dandy sleigh,
An' if that's all you want ter know
    I'll skip along an' play.

If Those Who Love Us

IF those who love us find us true
And kind and gentle, and are glad
When each grim working day is through
To have us near them, why be sad?

If those who know us best rejoice
In what we are and hold us dear,
What matter if the stranger's voice
Shall speak the bitter jibe and jeer?

If those who cling to us still smile
Though grim misfortune has us down,
If they still think our work worth while,
What matters it if strangers frown?

The Simple Toilers

JUST to do the little things
And do them well from day to day,
Enough of satisfaction brings
To those who tread the simple way;
To make the striving here worth while
They do not ask for glories great,
They're happy with the rank and file
And are content to work and wait.

They seek their homes at close of day
And there find happiness and rest,
They watch their little children play,
And out of life they draw the best.
All unafraid they view the sun
Sink out of sight and night descend,
They miss the cares when day is done,
The sleepless hours that fame attend.

175

Friendship

YOU can buy, if you've got money, all you need
  to drink and eat,
    You can pay for bread and honey, and can
keep your palate sweet.
But when trouble comes to fret you, and when sorrow
  comes your way,
For the gentle hand of friendship that you need you
  cannot pay.

You can buy with gold and silver things you've got to
  have to wear,
You can purchase all that's needful, when your skies
  are bright and fair;
But when clouds begin to gather and when trouble
  rules the day
Your money doesn't lure a friend worth while to come
  your way.

For the hand that's warm and gripping and the heart's
  that tender, too,
Are what all men living sigh for when they're sorrowful
  and blue,
For there's nothing that's so soothing and so comfort-
  ing right then
As the gladly given friendship of a fellow's fellow men.

A hand upon your shoulder and a whispered word of
  cheer
Are the things that keep you going when your trouble
  time is here;
And you'll hate the gold you've gathered and the
  buildings that you own
If you have to bear your troubles and your sorrows all
  alone.

If you've served a golden idol you will get as your
  reward
All the luxuries of living that the coins of gold afford,

But you'll be the poorest mortal and the saddest in the
     end
When the clouds of trouble gather—and you're hungry
     for a friend.

The Cure

WHEN you can't get her out of your head, young
     man,
     And you hate what you have to do;
And you shirk every task that you find you can,
     And the others you hurry through.
When all you can see is the time to quit,
     (I know how each symptom goes),
There's only one way to get over it,
     The next time you see her—propose.

When you think when you're called to the telephone
     That hers is the voice you'll hear,
And because it isn't, you sigh and groan;
     When you find that your brain's not clear
And you can't add figures or write a bit
     When the columns are all awhirl,
There's only one way to get over it,
     And that is to marry the girl.

The Baby's Feet

PINKER than the roses that enrich a summer's
day,
 Splashing in the bath tub or just kicking
 them in play,
Nothing in the skies above or earth below as sweet,
As fascinating to me as a baby's little feet.

Every toe a rosebud, on a chubby, dimpled tree,
Little legs as rounded and as plump as they can be,
Peeping through the nighties, or kicking in the air,
Angel wings aren't prettier than baby's feet, I swear.

Not a sign of travel, not a sign of care,
Not a sign of burdens they have had to bear,
Just the pinkest pinkness and the plumpest plumpness
 known,
Kicking in their gladness when the covers back are
 thrown.

Little feet that never yet have stepped aside to sin,
Never trampled others down in selfishness to win,
Never felt the bruises or the weariness of strife,
Aren't they good to look at as they're starting out in
 life?

Little feet, I wonder, as I watch you kick in play,
Peeping through your nightie at the ending of the day,
Wonder where you'll wander in the years that lie
 ahead,
And I pray the Lord to guard you o'er the paths that
 you must tread.

A Lullaby

THE dream ship is ready, the sea is like gold
    And the fairy prince waits in command;
    There's a cargo of wonderful dreams in the
      hold,
For the baby that seeks Slumberland.
There are fairies in pink and good fairies in white,
    A watch o'er the baby to keep,
Now the silver sails fill with the breeze of the night,
    All aboard, for the Harbor of Sleep!

I pray that no tempest shall ruffle the sea
    Through the long night that he is away;
And I pray the good captain will bring him to me
    With a smile at the close of the day.
Oh, soft as his breath be the breezes that blow,
    And gentle the long waves that sweep
The wonderful ship that is waiting to go
    With my babe to the Harbor of Sleep.

Softly, so softly, the ship slips away
    With its silver sails catching the breeze,
The stars in the sky seem to twinkle and say
    Our watch we will keep o'er the seas.
And never a tempest shall happen this night,
    But peace shall slip down on the deep,
Safe and sound shall return, with the coming of light,
    Your babe from the Harbor of Sleep.

The Brave Men

HERE'S to the men who laugh
    In the face of grim despair,
    Who gather the tares and chaff
But sow with a cheerful air.
Here's to the smiling men
    Who, giving, can take a blow,
And rise to the fight again
    When others have laid them low.

Here's to the men who grin
    When plans that they build go wrong,
And straightway new plans begin
    With courage and purpose strong.
Here's to the glad, brave men
    Who, battling, expect a bruise,
And rise to the fight again
    Undaunted by fights they lose.

Here's to the men who smile,
    With faith in the morning light,
And bravely await the while
    Till victory crowns their fight.
Here's to the fighting men
    That always need not succeed,
To rise to the fight again—
    The brave in defeat we need.

Little Fellow

OH, you laughing little fellow, with your eyes
    agleam with fun,
      And your golden curls a-mockin' all the
      splendor of the sun,
With your cheeks a wee bit redder than the petals
    of the rose,
You don't know just what you mean to your daddy,
    I suppose.

With your rompin' and your shoutin' an' your laughin'
    through the day,
You've no care of what's before you, what lies yonder
    down the way;
Why, your little brain is whirlin' with the gladness
    of the earth,
An' of course you have no notion of how much to me
    you're worth.

Jes' keep laughin', little fellow, keep those eyes agleam
    with fun,
Jes' keep rompin' in the meadows an' a-dancin' in
    the sun,
For the bloom of health upon you is the thing I want
    to see,
Coz, you bright-eyed little fellow, you are all the
    world to me.

The Lilacs

IT'S hard to find fault with the world
  With the lilacs in bloom at the door,
    Then the banners of Grouchdom are furled
  And life is worth living once more,
The loved ones gone yonder come back
  To breathe once again their perfume,
And joy has a clear, open track
  With the old-fashioned lilacs in bloom.

We all are together again,
  The mother that loved them is here;
The grandfather taps with his cane
  The walks that he once held so dear.
The family circle is whole
  And sunshine has banished the gloom,
And memories sweet flood the soul,
  With the old-fashioned lilacs in bloom.

Home is nearer to Heaven it seems,
  And the stream that divides not so vast;
For we live once again in our dreams
  The scenes of our sanctified past.
And back to us come in a troop
  The loved ones, asleep in the tomb,
To sit for a while on the stoop
  With the old-fashioned lilacs in bloom.

Success

SUCCESS is not in getting rich,
　　'Tis not in winning fame;
　　Tis not in climbing from the ditch
　　To gain the world's acclaim.
'Tis not in leading armies strong,
　　For he's successful, too,
Who brings his best the whole day long
　　To what he has to do.

The humble toiler in the field
　　Who tends his acres small
And watches them that they may yield
　　Their utmost in the fall
Has just as much of right to boast
　　As he whom thousands cheer,
For he has also made the most
　　Of what God gave him here.

The man who does his duty well,
　　Although his task be small,
And in a cottage poor he dwell
　　Successful we should call.
If he has given his task the best
　　He had, nor ever swerved
From what is right, he's met the test.
　　Success is having served.

Pa Discusses Economy

"THIS year," said Pa, on New Year's night,
　　　"we'll start upon a different plan,
　　　I'm sick and tired of ending years as poor
　　　　　as when those years began;
I'm sick and tired of spending coin before I've really
　　　got it earned,
This year we're going to save some dough—that is the
　　　new leaf that I've turned."

Ma didn't say a word right then, an' Pa went on:
　　　"This year we'll try
To cut out all our foolishness, an' put a little money
　　　by;
It's terrible the way we've spent the money that I
　　　labor for
On things that we don't really need, but we won't do
　　　it any more.

"There's lots of ways that we can save, we'll stop the
　　　many little leaks
And soon we'll have a bank account—I've thought it
　　　out for weeks and weeks;
I'm sick and tired of toiling hard, an' havin' nothing
　　　left to show
For all I've done the long year through—this year
　　　we'll start to save our dough."

An' Ma looked up an' said to Pa, "I'm glad to hear
　　　you make that vow,
We ought to save a lot each year; an' listen while I
　　　tell you how:
Those poker games you ought to stop, I've always
　　　said that they're not right,
Ten dollars that we could have saved you lost at
　　　Brown's the other night.

"An' then you cut out shaking dice with friends who
　　　ride in motor cars,
We'd save a lot of coin if you'd quit getting stuck for
　　　their cigars;

184

There are a lot of ways to save our money I can
   plainly see."
Then Pa got mad an' said, "That's right, I knew
   you'd blame it all on me."

After All Is Said and Done

AFTER all is said and done,
      After all the work and fun,
      After all the sighing's over
And the laughter fades away,
Then the cares that now beset us
And the little wrongs that fret us
Will diminish in their value
As we sail across the bay.

There will be no friends departed,
There will be no heavy-hearted,
There will be no looking backward
To the joys of long ago;
There will be no sad words spoken
In a voice that's low and broken
Of the loved ones that are missing
And the joys we used to know.

After all is said and done,
After all the work and fun,
We shall be once more united,
With our sorrows swept away;
Each new day will bring its pleasure
In a splendid heaping measure,
And no one of us shall sigh for
Any by-gone yesterday.

The Home-Wrecker

MISCHIEVOUS and full of fun,
    Eyes that sparkle like the sun;
    Mouth that's always in a smile,
Hands in trouble all the while.
Tugging this and tugging that,
Nothing that you don't get at,
Nothing that you do not do,
Roguish little tyke of two.

Prying round the house you go,
Everything you want to know,
Everything you want to see,
Bunch of curiosity.
Nothing's safe with you about,
Nothing you don't ferret out.
"No! No's!" do not hinder you,
Roguish little tyke of two.

All day long you tear and break,
Ruin follows in your wake,
Just as though the tables are
Made for little feet to mar;
Just as though I spend my cash
For pottery for you to smash;
You're destructive through and through,
Roguish little tyke of two.

Hands and feet are never still,
Ink you think is made to spill;
On from this to that you pass
To the sound of falling glass.
Cups, you think, were made to throw
On the hardwood floor below.
Gleefully their wreck you view,
Roguish little tyke of two.

But I'd rather have it so,
Than the home I used to know;
Rather have you crash and break,
Leaving ruin in your wake;

Rather have you tug and tear
Till the place is worn and bare,
Than the childless home I knew,
Roguish little tyke of two.

A Father's Thought

THEY say the little fellow looks like me,
But I'm hoping he'll be better
than I've been,
And I'm hoping and I'm planning that he'll see
A little more of sunshine than I've seen.
Oh, I sit and watch him there,
Smiling at me from his chair,
And I'm dreaming of the days that are to be;
And I'm hoping he'll attain
All the goals I couldn't gain
In the years when he is treading after me.

He's exactly like his father, so I'm told,
But I'm hoping he will be a better man;
On what I may gain of glory or of gold
I have ceased to give my effort or to plan.
Through the boy who looks like me
I've another chance to be
A credit to myself, and so I say
If I can but see him gain
What I never could attain,
At the end, without regrets, I'll pass away.

If You and I

IF you would smile a little more
    And I would kinder be,
    If you would stop to think before
    You speak of faults you see.
If I would show more patience, too,
    With all with whom I'm hurled,
Then I would help and so would you
    To make a better world.

If you would cheer your neighbor more
    And I'd encourage mine,
If you would linger at his door
    To say his work is fine, .
And I would stop to help him when
    His lips in frowns are curled,
Both you and I'd be helping then
    To make a better world.

But just as long as you keep still
    And plod your selfish way,
And I rush on, and heedless kill
    The kind words I could say;
While you and I refuse to smile
    And keep our gay flags furled,
Someone will grumble all the while
    That it's a gloomy world.

CPSIA information can be obtained
at www.ICGtesting.com
Printed in the USA
LVHW081538030721
691838LV00002B/170